marxi

in today'...orld

marxism
in today's world

peter taaffe

answers on war, capitalism and environment
the committee for a workers' international

Published by the Committee for a Workers' International (CWI)

November 2006

Marxism in Today's World
Peter Taaffe
© CWI Publications and Socialist Publications Ltd 2006

First Edition November 2006

Classification: Peter Taaffe
History/Politics/Economics/Sociology

ISBN 1-870958-32-2 pbk
EAN-13 978-1-870958-32-2 pbk

A catalogue record for this book is available from the British Library
Published by the Committee for a Workers' International (CWI)
www.socialistworld.net
Typeset in Utopia 9 pt
Printed by Russell Press (Nottingham)

**Distribution by Socialist Books,
PO Box 24697, London, E11 1YD
Telephone +44 (0)20 8988 8789
e-mail: bookshop@socialistparty.org.uk
www.socialistbooks.co.uk**

typesetting & design: dennis@kavitagraphics.co.uk

marxism
in today's world
peter taaffe

answers on war, capitalism and environment
the committee for a workers' international

Acknowledgements

Preface and Acknowledgements

This book arose from a request to the Committee for a Workers' International (CWI) by an Italian publishing collective 'Giovane Talpa' for information about our ideas and policies with a view to publishing a book in Italy outlining the policies of the CWI.

As well as supplying documents and newspapers of the CWI and its national sections, it was subsequently agreed that representatives of Giovane Talpa would visit London for discussions with the CWI. They suggested that, during the visit, they would interview me, Peter Taaffe, speaking on behalf of the CWI. Yurii Colombo was able to visit London and the interview was conducted between 21 and 25 September 2006. Also present was Bob Labi. I answered most of Yurii's questions but there were some important observations by Bob, which we publish alongside my comments.

We hope that the reader will agree that the format of this book – of questions and answers on a whole range of historical and contemporary issues – allows us to explain and clarify our ideas in some detail. The manner of presentation and also the sequence in which arguments are presented can pose for the reader some problems of a stylistic character. However, we have decided to maintain this format, because it gives an authentic 'feel' to the kind of discussion of our ideas, including interjections, which took place.

Once we read the whole transcript of these discussions, we decided that, in addition to Giovane Talpa publishing the book in Italian, we would issue an English version as well. This was in agreement with Giovane Talpa. We are extremely grateful to them, particularly Yurii, for suggesting this initiative and implementing it. Discussion and the debate of ideas through exchanges like this, conducted in a comradely way, are vital in this period of growing political ferment but also of doubts and questioning in the workers' movement internationally.

Such is the speed of events today in the world of globalised neo-liberal capitalism, that what is written one day can very quickly be overtaken, sometimes in a matter of weeks or months. However, we have resisted the temptation to add additional points about events which took place after the original interview was conducted, apart from the occasional note to clarify issues.

I am extremely grateful to Kevin Parslow who has, as ever, been indefatigable in typing, at short notice, this lengthy 'interview'. He has also assiduously checked out important facts. I would also like to thank Manny Thain for typing part of the interview and proofreading, Tony Saunois, Bob Labi and Clare Doyle for reading and checking what is presented here. Other comrades have also read parts of the interview. Any mistakes which remain, I am responsible for. We would welcome comments and discussion about the ideas of the CWI presented here.

Peter Taaffe
October 2006

Twin towers erupt in flames on 9/11

9/11 and After

What are the changes in the world situation since the 9/11 attacks?

9/11 was undoubtedly a worldwide turning point. It gave US imperialism, through the presidency of George W Bush, the opportunity to actually implement long-discussed policies of its neo-liberal wing. Their plans go back ten years before 9/11 with the ideas of people like Richard Perle and Paul Wolfowitz outlined in the 'Project for a New American Century'. The elements of that policy were for a new assertive hegemonic world role for US imperialism. They were looking for a pretext to use the colossal military might that US imperialism had accumulated.

Because American imperialism is the only real superpower on the world arena at the present time, with the demise of the Soviet Union, the neo-conservative wing of American capitalism was concerned that this power was not being effectively used to enhance its world position. The pretext for achieving this was, of course, 9/11. Evidence has been produced since then which shows that the neo-conservatives around figures like Donald Rumsfeld and Wolfowitz were, in the first few hours after 9/11, actually trying to convince Bush to use the attack not to invade Afghanistan in the first instance but to go after Saddam Hussein.

Their plans were temporarily thwarted by those like Colin Powell and the more 'cautious' wing of the American bourgeoisie. Powell argued that if Osama bin Laden was proven to be the organiser of the attack on the twin towers, if then this incident was utilised to attack Iraq, this would not be seen as legitimate in the eyes of either the American people or the rest of the world. That is why, amongst other reasons, they decided to attack al-Qa'ida's base in Afghanistan. This facilitated a change to a more assertive role for US imperialism. However, we should not forget that the Clinton administration was also interventionist in the 1990s, bombing Serbia/Kosova, as well as Sudan. But it was not as naked or as brutal as the Bush regime. The Clinton administration tried to cover up the role of US imperialism under (Woodrow) Wilsonian 'liberalism', capitalist 'humanitarianism'. Clinton sought to go through multilateral agencies like the United Nations wherever that was possible. Bush brutally broke away from this in the aftermath of 9/11 and it created a new world situation.

In the aftermath of 9/11, we produced a lot of analytical material (available on the CWI website) in which we pointed out that US imperialism would adopt a pre-emptive strategy bolstered by its military prowess; it now accounts for 50% of world arms expenditure. There has never been a military power with such dominance in the history of the world, not even during the 'Cold War'. Then Stalinism counter-balanced the US. So this was a new situation.

The US was initially successful in the war in Afghanistan largely because the forces which they faced, the Taliban, refused to fight before the war had got under way. It was an easy victory. It actually fostered the idea that it was possible to gain a victory by air power alone. Yet the whole of history in the modern era has shown that, by itself, air power alone is not sufficient to guarantee a military victory. That was underlined by the events in Lebanon during the course of the recent war. After Afghanistan, in a quite blatant fashion, the ground was prepared for an intervention in Iraq.

Many people, including some who were Marxists and Trotskyists, were blown off course, destabilised or disorientated by the events of 9/11. There was pessimism in the neo-colonial world and the advanced industrial countries that this colossal power of US imperialism could be defeated. Afghanistan was the third war which they had won after the Gulf War of the early 1990s and Kosova. It looked as though the American juggernaut was unstoppable from a military point of view. The evidence was there which appeared to show that. We went to great pains in the documents of the Committee for a Workers' International (CWI) to show the limits of that power. It is one thing to defeat a discredited regime like Saddam Hussein's in the 1991 Gulf War after he occupied Kuwait. World public opinion was against him. But Iraq in 2001 was a different proposition because what was being proposed was not just the use of air power or a police-type operation but a full military invasion and occupation.

A big discussion took place in our ranks on whether it was possible for Bush junior to go ahead with the invasion. The American bourgeoisie was split on this issue. In fact, even the Republican Party establishment did not believe that Bush would be prepared to actually engage in this war. We predicted that if he did invade, the USA would be drawn into a quagmire. We used the example of Vietnam as a warning to the US. It has some application to Iraq but there are also some profound differences. So the situation following 9/11 represented a big change. It underlined the fact that the US was the mightiest power militarily on the globe. It would use 9/11 to enhance its position and change the balance of forces in its favour, and seek to reverse all the defeats, if it could, which it suffered in the past. It wanted to destroy the 'Vietnam syndrome' which existed in the US peoples' consciousness; that never again should a US foreign military invasion and occupation be launched. The Iraq War was deliberately framed to break that and to some extent it appeared originally as though that had been achieved. But we predicted that there would be Arab nationalist resistance in Iraq, irrespective of Saddam Hussein.

You said the left after 9/11 was confused and did not understand well what was happening. It was quite clear that until the summer of 2002 the anti-globalisation movement was growing very quickly. Afterwards, there were other big demonstrations but the movement began to decline after 9/11 and after that there was a rightward movement. But I think the anti-war movement before the Iraq War was something different from the anti-globalisation movement. The movement in Italy was very big, not only the people who participated in the meetings, actions, etc, but in the general mass...for example, we had the experience of flags in windows everywhere; 'peace, peace, peace', in their millions. You can still see thousands today when you arrive in Italy. But after a downturn in the movement when the war began, they realised they could not stop the war. The reformist parties began to say, yes we were against the war but now there is a war and we are for democracy, for a new society in Iraq and for democratisation but we are against the occupation. What do you think about the situation in general of the anti-globalisation and anti-war movement?

We would agree with your general point, which affects not only Italy but has a general relevance to the anti-war movement internationally. The anti-globalisation movement went through ups and downs. In the first instance it was a reaction against capitalist globalisation worldwide, the neo-liberal policies that went with it and the threat of war, destruction of the environment, etc. In the aftermath of 9/11 there was shock. Let us remember that the European bourgeoisie was initially uncritical of US imperialism, summed up quite dramatically in a headline in *Le Monde* which said: 'We are all Americans now'. This was a huge departure from the usual critical stance of the majority of the European bourgeoisie and particularly the French bourgeoisie towards the US. 9/11 did allow the relatively quick victory in Afghanistan. There was not the same reaction to this event even in the anti-war movement which was at quite a low ebb in Britain. But with Iraq and the lead-up to the war, which was quite protracted, it became clear that Bush and Blair were telling lies about weapons of mass destruction. There was growing bitterness and anger, and a complete swing in public opinion against the war, although the mood differed from country to country.

In the US, because of the enormous power of the media and of the presidency, as well as the Democrats' capitulation to Bush, there was an overwhelming majority in favour of the war. There was also a significant minority opposed. But the majority said, 'Well, we have had a quick victory in Afghanistan, our troops are there, so we should support them.' In addition, there is always the tendency for the population to support 'our troops' in the first instance, even when they are critical of a war. That then turns into its opposite if the war goes badly, as is the case with Iraq today. But a huge movement built up against the Iraq War which culminated in the 15 February 2003 worldwide demonstrations. In London, we had the biggest demonstration in history, bigger than the anti-poll tax demonstration, larger than the Chartists' demonstrations of the first half of the 19th century. It reflected the fact that the overwhelming majority of the population was opposed to the war. In fact, Blair actually discussed with his own family, it has been revealed since, that he would probably have to resign from the government, such was the huge wellspring of opposition to the war from below in Britain.

There were ebbs and flows even in this movement. Once the war began, even though two million had demonstrated, a certain acquiescence set in. One of the reasons the movement did not succeed was its one-dimensional pacifist character, not just of the people who participated – it is natural that workers and the middle class would immediately, in the first instance, say 'we want peace' – but of its leaders as well. The leaders of the anti-war movement in Britain kept the movement within very narrow limits. Some did pose the question of a general strike but in a very demagogic fashion. You cannot just organise a general strike on the question of war without serious preparation. Because of that, although opposition to the war has grown, the anti-war movement in the immediate aftermath of the invasion of Iraq was not as large as before. Since then, it has gone through a number of ebbs and flows, as the situation has worsened in Iraq.

There exists a paradoxical situation now. There is greater opposition to the war in the US and Britain in particular. The majority is now opposed to the war. There are overwhelming majorities against the war in Europe and yet the participation in the anti-war demonstrations is not on the level that it was in 2003. Why? It is because there is a feeling that demonstrations, in and of themselves, are not sufficient. We need to get rid of the pro-war government – or at least the leaders like Blair – we need a clear class policy to take the anti-war movement forward.

A US Conspiracy?

The second question may be strange but deals with the decline of the movement. In the last months there have been many books, discussions on the internet and also, two weeks ago in Milan, 150 people attended a film which claimed that the US organised 9/11 themselves or that they knew, like

Pearl Harbor when it was known the Japanese would attack. What do you think of this theory? Is it a sign of the decline of the anti-war movement and what do you think about terrorism?

I would not necessarily say it was a manifestation of the decline of the anti-war movement because there is a lot of *prima facie* evidence that US imperialism was hoping and preparing for some kind of event like 9/11. As we said earlier, this would give them the pretext to realise the international programme of neo-liberalism. However, I do not think, unless there is conclusive evidence to the contrary, that this was the same as Pearl Harbor. There is an ongoing controversy over this event, but most people who have examined the situation at the time of Pearl Harbor would agree and have understood that Japanese imperialism was manoeuvred into the war by US imperialism. Japan relied on oil and this was choked off by the US, forcing Japan to resort to war. US imperialism had prepared the ground for some kind of attack by Japan which would give them the excuse to enter the Second World War. That is the most likely scenario of what happened around Pearl Harbor. I agree with Gore Vidal, the American writer, who has produced some very telling material on this.

If you look at the run-up to 9/11, given the warnings even two months before the event, you could say there is some evidence to suggest that American imperialism as a whole, or an agency of American imperialism such as the CIA or some secret service, or Mossad in combination with American imperialism, prepared for this particular incident. I do not think it is the same as Pearl Harbor, however. There is a lot of circumstantial evidence which shows that the Bush regime took its eye off the ball, was not vigilant, did not consider that Osama bin Laden would be able to carry through an attack of this kind. Therefore it is very unlikely that the US or its agencies were behind this attack. We will only be able to know for certain what the truth is when the secret files are released.

What is true is the majority of the Muslims in the Middle East and worldwide believes that 9/11 was a conscious plot organised by American imperialism in conjunction with Mossad. That is partly because they do not like to think that Muslims could have taken this kind of indiscriminate, murderous action. But I would say that this was an action by al-Qa'ida. It was also revenge, a nemesis, for American imperialism which had created al-Qa'ida in the first instance in Afghanistan. They created a Frankenstein's monster which came back to haunt them in the attack of 9/11.

The most important thing is what flowed from this event. It has shaped the current situation which has given American militarism and imperialism this opportunity to enhance its material forces to intervene in Iraq. This, in turn, has polarised the situation in the Middle East and elsewhere, where the impression is that Islam is under attack. This has given right-wing political Islam a new lease of life in the Middle East and elsewhere.

You said before that US military spending is now more than all the other countries of the world and you stated that it is the only world superpower. But in your last article and documents you speak about the decline of the US. How do you connect these different statements and explain this relationship?

American imperialism is still the major military power and up to now is still the major economic power, although it has experienced a process of deindustrial-isation similar to the whole of Western Europe. In fact, while there still is an important industrial proletariat in Western Europe, nevertheless, one of the consequences of globalisation is the outsourcing of industry, partly to Eastern Europe but in the main to China, a shift in the location of the majority of Marx's industrial proletariat from the 'West' to the 'East', which is now the 'workshop of the world'.

This raises important issues for Marxists for the future. There is the enormous weight of American imperialism militarily and still economically but without the same kind of underlying economic national strength which it had in the past. In 1945, most of the gold in the world was concentrated in Fort Knox and 50% of world production came from the US. In the last two decades, however, there has been a steady decline in the share of domestic industrial production in the US. The result is that America has ballooning deficits including a negative balance of trade on the current account. It has gone from being the major creditor nation and the banker of the world to the biggest debtor nation and is being propped up by Asian capitalism, particularly China.

US capitalism will be caught in a contradiction in the next period. The huge military power and economic weight of the US is increasingly financed by the rest of the world. If the US was any other economy, Italy or Britain for instance, with a 7% deficit on its current account, then the IMF would go in, declare the country bankrupt and introduce an austerity programme! But paradoxically and dialectical-ly, because of the world role of US imperialism, it is using its economic weakness and its military might to hold the rest of the world to ransom to force others to finance this deficit and to give it the leeway to enhance its power internationally. Chalmers Johnson, a perceptive bourgeois commentator on the 'American Empire', in a recent book made the point that America is now an "imperialism of bases". It has 725 acknowledged bases throughout the world. But, in reality, it has an astonishing 1,400 in total. Once it establishes a base, it generally never retreats from it. The only case in the post-war period – apart from China following the revolution – where it retreated was at Clark Base in the Philippines because of the revolution there which resulted in the overthrow of Marcos. But in the aftermath of 9/11 they have been allowed back and have now reoccupied the base! So there is this enormous web internationally, linked to the material interests of US imperialism but accompanied by a growing underlying economic weakness.

The limits on American imperialism on the international arena have been shown in Iraq, and also by Somalia in the recent period. Clinton intervened in 1993-94 but American troops were forced to withdraw. Bush has been pursuing a proxy war in Somalia. The government was defeated by the Islamic courts and now we have an Islamic state. The US is now trying to get Ethiopia to attack Somalia. Internationally, everywhere, the US now finds itself if not yet defeated then certainly weakened.

In the US itself, Hurricane Katrina revealed the economic and social ulcer at the heart of American imperialism. Trotsky predicted in the 1930s, in relation to the likely outcome of the looming Second World War, the US would come out of the war as the strongest power worldwide but it would build into its foundations all the combustible material, all the explosive factors of world capitalism. We saw that with Korea, Vietnam and now with Iraq. In effect, the international role of US imperialism will feed into and reinforce its economic decline. This decline is relative at the present time. Will it become an absolute decline and what will be the consequences of that? That is another issue, related to the rise of China and the geopolitical, as well as economic, competition, in particular, of China to American imperialism.

'European bloc' and unification

In the European reformist left and in the left in general there is big anti-Americanism and big support for a strong Europe because European states are more humane, their international politics are more pacifistic and we have a longer tradition of culture than the US. Public opinion says we need a strong Europe as a counterweight to the US. Now many people say that the most radical wing of the anti-globalisation movement has been supported by the result of the French referendum. What do you think about European unification and the growth of this kind of ideology in the left, of anti-Americanism but pro-European imperialist? And most importantly, do you think that it is possible under capitalism to achieve the unification of Europe because we saw the referendums in France and Netherlands stopping the

**process but also during the Iraq War it was supported by right-wing govern-
ments such as Britain, Spain and Italy, and many Eastern European states.
So there was a split inside Europe. What do you think of these questions?**

The short answer to the possibility of complete European unification under
capitalism is a straight no. The second question: because of the opposition of
Europe's population and some of the capitalist governments of Europe, should we
be in favour of a bloc between capitalist Europe and China, Russia, etc, against the
US? Our answer to that would also be no. This is because we believe the working
class on all questions should take an independent class position. We cannot support
bourgeois governments when they pretend to or appear to be representing the
'interests' of Europeans. We have to point to the real intentions of the European
bourgeoisie.

If you look at the split between Europe and the US which took place on the question
of the war, it was partly a reflection of the mood of the populations of Europe. It was
not an accident that Aznar in Spain supported the war, while his population was
opposed, and in the aftermath of the Madrid bombing he was thrown out of office.
Berlusconi supported the war and, by a narrow majority it is true, he was ejected
from office. Now Blair is about to depart from the scene in Britain in the next weeks
or months. One of the reasons for their demise was their support for the war. On the
other hand, the French bourgeois government and Schröder in Germany, while
being right wing on domestic policy, carrying through neo-liberal programmes, at
the same time took up anti-war postures internationally which were reflections of
the domestic moods in these countries. The governments of Central Europe such as
Poland and elsewhere supported the US in the war – but even in those cases big
sections or majorities in society were moving in opposition to the war.

Two processes took place. There was an inter-imperialist rivalry between some of
the dominant regimes of Europe and the US. Britain is a bit of an exception – there
has been an Anglo-US bloc particularly since the Suez adventure of 1956. After
this, the British bourgeoisie decided that they could not afford to be in opposition
to US imperialism. Since then, the so-called 'special relationship' has existed. But
that did not stop Harold Wilson, the Labour prime minister in the 1960s, saying
'no' to President Johnson's request for British troops in Vietnam. Why? Because his
cabinet would have split apart because of the mass opposition to the war and the
different character of the Labour Party then. Blair's New Labour party is a
bourgeois party. With no pressure from 'below' – there is no working-class base in
the party – he was able to defy public opinion for a period. Because of this alleged
special relationship, his government supported US imperialism.

So there was a split between sections of the European bourgeoisie and the US, and also a split within Europe. That is a political split with economic roots as well. We have always opposed even some Marxists and Trotskyists who in the past had the attitude that it was possible in the new era of imperialism for Europe to be united on a capitalist basis. We stand by the original analysis of Marxism, of Trotsky in particular, that capitalism cannot fully overcome the problems of the nation state. Capital in the modern era is not borderless – ultimately it rests on a base in one country or another. The amalgamation internationally into transnationals has been taken a long way; the unification of Europe, in one sense, went a lot further, with tariff barriers coming down, with the creation of the European parliament, etc. We argued when we were part of the United Secretariat of the Fourth International (USFI) up to 1965 that it could go perhaps a long way towards unification but could not go that extra 10% or so to complete the process.

Capitalism cannot overcome the narrow limits of the nation state and organise the productive forces on a European level while at the same time creating a political unification of the European bourgeoisie. Now the contradictions, in this period of intense international economic competition, have come to the fore. It was shown in the European referendums in France and the Netherlands with the rejection of the European constitution. It was correct to vote against the EU constitution; the French working class understood that this was a step towards further neo-liberal policies. This constitution is so long that very few people have read it! Even the European legislators have not read this constitution, it is so obscure! It is, moreover, like the original Treaty of Rome, which in effect tries to permanently enshrine capitalism. The proposed constitution was an extension of that on a European-wide level. We are opposed to that. It gives legal sanction to privatisation and neo-liberal policies, and is also a step, if they could get away with it, to the organisation of European capitalism against the working class.

So it is not possible for capitalism to overcome the narrow limits of the nation state. They can partially create a European capital market; they have created a customs union. But in the battle over the European services directive and on a whole number of other issues, it has shown that it is very difficult to take that extra step towards the unification of the European bourgeoisie. In other words, I believe in Trotsky's original analysis in its broad outline that the only way that Europe could be unified from the 'Urals to the Atlantic' is by the European working class acting together to establish socialism on a continental scale. We stand for the unification of Europe. We are opposed to a narrow capitalist nationalist opposition to Europe and we oppose those who support right-wing nationalist parties in a common bloc against the unification of Europe. We are in favour of a working-class alternative, the idea of a Europe of the working class, of a united socialist states of Europe, the original slogan of the Communist International which is still valid today.

Two million march against war in London 15 February 2003

The World Situation

Like the majority of Marxists internationally you say there was a change in economics in the mid-1970s. Before, we had a very long period of development of capitalism worldwide, not only in the advanced countries but also the beginning of national liberation movements. But after the mid-1970s a new cycle of capitalism began. The world upswing was finished and the problems of oil began. But we as Marxists have had experience of a crisis of capitalism and crisis of revolutionary processes very near together. There was a crisis, and after, an upsurge of the revolutionary movement but not the definite crisis of capitalism or worldwide revolution. For example, in the period between the First and Second World Wars the contradiction and crisis became very deep and had only two solutions: war or revolution, or after a war, revolution. We see today two tiers in worldwide capitalism. What characteristic today is different to the crisis before the Second World War, the changes to regulation of crises and why did we have deep clashes between the imperialist forces in the Second World War? For example, you say that US imperialist forces are so strong militarily that other countries do not try to defeat it. But also Hitler was clear that the US could not be beaten but he tried to think about a European war.

This is a very big subject so we can only give the main points but it is a key question for understanding the past but also the current situation. Firstly, the period following the Second World War was different to that following the First World War, as you pointed out. The period from 1918 to 1938 was, in general, a period of economic stagnation punctuated by the most serious economic crash in the history of capitalism (1929-33). Unemployment rose to 25% of the labour force in the US and a fall of 50% in the national income of the strongest power on the planet. It was a period of revolution and counter-revolution which culminated in the Second World War. The period that followed the Second World War was similar in one sense: out of the Second World War came a revolutionary wave, starting in Italy in 1943-44 with the overthrow of Mussolini. There were revolutionary events in France where the French working class in Paris defeated the forces of the Nazis, when de Gaulle was 50 miles from Paris, and there was the opportunity for another Paris Commune. But the Communist Party stepped in and stopped it. In Britain, there was the election of a majority Labour government for the first time in history. In Italy, the period of the popular front. All of that reflected a revolutionary wave, which was similar in many respects to the post-1918 situation.

Trotsky was right in his predictions of revolution following the war. But he could not foresee that Stalinism and social democracy would save capitalism with a series of popular front governments in France and Italy, the crushing of the revolution in Greece, the Labour government in Britain which carried through a quarter of a revolution, nationalising basic infrastructures. They saved capitalism. In a way, it was a counter-revolution in a democratic form, not by the mailed fist of dictatorship. Having saved capitalism, together with new economic factors, it laid the basis for one of the greatest upswings in the history of capitalism from 1950-74/75.

The main causes of that were the enormous destruction from the war including the proletariat, its labour power, in a sense the liquidation of 'variable' capital, as well as the destruction of 'constant' capital, together with new techniques in electronics, plastics. This all came together in a spiral effect, which led to the upswing of world capitalism. The Revolutionary Communist Party (RCP) in Britain was probably the first to recognise that, whereas the Fourth International's leadership had the perspective of an immediate crisis. The Revolutionary Communist Party said that was not going to happen because the political preconditions had been created for this economic upswing. But even the RCP did not expect that the boom would go on for so long and have such a big effect.

This boom, a structural upswing of capitalism, because that is what it was, increased living standards significantly. There was not just the growth of industry in general but also a growth of the working class and growing real living standards. Even some of the crumbs off the rich table of Europe, Japan and America went to the neo-colonial world. An analysis of what happened then is very important for understanding the current situation. The idea then developed, and it still holds sway, that this was the 'norm', the future for capitalism. There is today a harkening back to this 'golden era' and the hope that it could return. But this was an exceptional period in the history of capitalism. The periods prior to the First World War, of 'liberalism', and now this era of neo-liberalism, are the 'norm'. The 1950-75 period was exceptional. A period stretching over 25 years is a long time in a man or woman's life, but it is a moment or half a minute in the life of a society, or in the life of a class.

But 1974/75 represented the high-water mark in the development of capitalism. We have to remember that since 1974/75, we have had a number of crises. The 1974/75 crisis was overcome, in a way a bit like what China is doing at the moment, by recycling petrodollars back to the US, as the oil revenue of the Gulf states was reinvested in the US, Europe, etc. What do you do, keep dollars in the bank? It was recycled back; enormous credit was pumped into the world capitalist system. So the system went on.

In 1987, there was another crisis, with the biggest collapse of the stock market since 1929. Some of our comrades then, such as the late Ted Grant, said that this was going to be another 1929. We disagreed. The reason for this was that, through the boom of 1950-75 and after, capitalism had built up a layer of reserves, of liquidity. Japanese and German capitalism, in particular, stepped in. They delayed the crisis until 1990, when there was a serious recession from 1990-92.

The 1990s

Then we witnessed the collapse of the Soviet Union, which dovetailed with an economic upswing in the 1990s, although this upswing, and the whole period from 1974 to today, does not have the same character as the growth in production of 1950-74/75. Present growth rates are, in general, half of what they were in that period. Productivity rates, despite the claims of US bourgeois economists, are less. We have given all the figures in our publications. The living standards of the proletariat, its relative share, have fallen back. This resulted from the collapse of the Soviet Union and the consequent move to the right of the trade union leaders, as well as the social democratic and Communist Party leaders. The working class was politically and, to some extent, in the trade union field thrown back. A brutal policy of neo-liberalism was carried through right up to the present period. This has altered the share going to the working classes, decreasing dramatically in some countries like Germany and the US, and is a world trend. It is true that the real living standards of a minority of the working class have gone up. But in America, for instance, median average earnings, of what they would call the 'middle class' – in reality, the upper layers of the working class – have stagnated or stood still throughout the whole of the 1990s. So this 'boom' or growth is a lopsided one. It is not the structural upswing that we saw from 1950 to 1975. And it is preparing the basis now, we believe, for a serious crisis, the timing of which, however, is very difficult to predict.

So our answer is that we have not had a 1929 crash for a combination of reasons. One factor in sustaining capitalism today is the collapse of the former Soviet Union and Eastern Europe and the growth of capitalism in China. According to *The Economist*, the world labour force is estimated to have doubled with the entry of China and Eastern Europe onto the world market and now stands between two and three billion. Therefore the opportunities for increased exploitation, what Marx called the expansion of the variable capital, labour power, have also increased. Cheap credit has been available, which has been assisted by the fact that, through the exploitation of the Chinese working class, in particular, inflation has been kept down. Cheap goods have flooded the markets of Western Europe, the US, Japan and the neo-colonial world. This has helped to hold down inflation. That, in turn, has had an effect on the rate of interest which has greatly depressed the inflationary tendencies which were a feature of capitalism in the 1970s.

All of these factors have had an effect. But, in a way, the most crucial point at the present time is the existence of a Faustian pact between emerging Chinese capitalism and US imperialism. The crux of the world economy today rests on an investment boom in China – mostly of foreign capital – and of a consumer boom in the US. Chinese capitalism has now built up a huge surplus. First of all, the balance of payments deficit in the US could be anything up to $725bn this year – as much as 7% of the gross domestic product (GDP). China has a trade surplus with the USA of $201bn. It has accumulated $1,000bn – *one trillion dollars* – of reserves, in paper dollars, for the goods that it has exported to the US. This build-up of dollar assets is used to plug the deficit of US imperialism. The problem is, how far does the gap expand before there is a 'bust'? From 7% to 8% to 9% to 10% before the holders of US dollars, not just China but South Korea and Asian capitalism as a whole, especially with the beginning of the decline of the dollar, say that is enough? This cheap credit has coalesced with a housing boom, which has allowed US house owners to take out loans; the whole mighty edifice of society has become indebted. The world economy is resting on 'chickens' legs', the US housing boom and the growing Chinese reserves.

It is only a matter of time before the dollar begins to decline. If you are holding huge reserves of dollars, what do you do? It is not rational to hold on to a currency when it looks as though it will decline. You begin to sell dollars, to exchange them for the euro, for instance. Once you start to buy euros, as South Korea did recently, the value of the euro goes up, the price of European exports goes up, which means that Europe's economic prospects would be profoundly affected. America, Europe and Japan would be seriously affected by this. The capitalists are on a merry-go-round. The Chinese dare not pull the plug on the dollar because that would immediately plunge the US and Europe into crisis. On the other hand, if they don't maintain the growth rate that they have in China now, they have a revolution. That's the dilemma. It is a most explosive situation that exists for world capitalism.

Growth rates this year, the real growth rates, are going ahead much more than even the capitalist experts expected. But often a flame flares up brightest just before it dies out. All the ingredients of a collapse are there but when it will happen, who knows? In the *Financial Times* recently there was a report of the collapse of a hedge fund valued at $6bn! And this evokes a shrug of their shoulders. The threat of a new Long Term Capital Management collapse, as in 1998, is not going to happen, they say. But then they make the point later on in the article that if four or five of these huge hedge funds go at once – bang!

But for the fact that in 1998 the New York wing of the US Federal Reserve stepped in and bailed out Long Term Capital Management, there would have been a financial crisis that would have had world repercussions, and may have led to a serious recession. You would not need a slump of the magnitude of 1929 to produce political convulsions like that today. Such is the development of the world productive forces a drop of a few percentage points in world output would have a colossal effect. In 1974-75, overall world GDP fell compared to the previous year (it almost halved) but there was still a small growth of 1.4%. However, industrial production fell by 1.6%. *The Economist* now suggests that world growth of less than 2% means an economic recession because this is the minimum growth required to prevent an increase in unemployment. In 1974, the small drop in industrial output, on top of the accumulated factors from the previous era had powerful world repercussions. It led to the revolutions in Spain, Portugal and Greece, and to the upheavals in France and Britain, which were a reflection, ultimately, of these economic processes. So the world economy, world capitalism, and perspectives for world capitalism, are a crucial question.

Nuclear threat

The second point raised is why have we not had clashes between the big imperialist forces as we had in the first half of the 20th century? One reason is the overwhelming dominance of American imperialism, militarily. The other factor is the world relationship of class forces and the pressure of the working class against war and for peace, which has been manifested in the huge anti-war demonstrations. This is a very important factor in checking the capitalists. The third factor, and as important, is of course that war between powerful states would not be on the lines of the Second World War because of the existence of nuclear weapons.

You could theoretically have a situation, and we even raised it in relation to Lebanon, if Israel was being defeated, or if there was an invasion of Iran and imperialist forces were being beaten, that sections of the American military and the Israeli ruling class may consider the use of tactical nuclear weapons. But the use of those weapons would provoke unprecedented mass opposition, even revolution. The revulsion today worldwide against what is happening in Iraq would be dwarfed if one power used tactical nuclear weapons in a conflict. It could lead to revolutionary convulsions, provoked by the prospect that the whole world was disintegrating because of the lunatics who are in power.

On the other hand, a nuclear Armageddon could not be ruled out theoretically if, for instance, a dictator took over in the US, smashed the unions, smashed democratic rights and so on. Faced with a military dictatorship like itself elsewhere which threatened it, theoretically you could not rule out that a US dictator might attempt a pre-emptive strike to destroy that regime. This is not a realistic perspective for the US or elsewhere in the foreseeable future. It would be absolutely mad for even the capitalists to go down this road. It is no accident that military experts dubbed the nuclear understanding between Stalinism and US imperialism 'MAD' - 'Mutually Assured Destruction'. Capitalism does not go to war for the sake of it but to conquer markets, to increase its income and so on. In destroying the working class, which is what would happen in a nuclear war, it would destroy the 'goose that lays the golden egg', the source of its profits and, thereby, its power. So we do not think that a general world war of a major inter-imperialist character is possible. Small wars or the kind of conflicts that we have seen in the 1990s involving American imperialism pitted against a national resistance movement; these are possible. A conflict over Taiwan between the US and China, and drawing in Japan, that is also a possibility. But it would stop short of the use of nuclear weapons. Regional wars, using conventional weapons, are also possible as the Israel-Lebanon conflict shows. A similar clash could develop between India and Pakistan.

But another, in a sense more important, 'war' could take place in the modern era, a trade war. This is really the modern form of war, because the lead up to an actual war, an armed conflict, is invariably preceded by an economic clash between the different powers. That was the reason for the First World War. It was the reason for the Second World War, as well. German capitalism was hemmed in and was seeking markets, colonies and so on in Eastern Europe at the expense of British imperialism.

The effects of the economic crisis on workers

There are two schools of thought we have to discuss in relation to the crisis of capitalism. On the one side, some people say the crisis begins, unemployment rises and there is a worsening of the situation. That is one thing. The second school said: No problem, now there is a crisis, but in two months we think there will be a recovery of the European economy, so also in Italy. The working class was silent in the period of crisis, because they did not want to lose work. They were afraid to struggle during the crisis. When it looks like the capitalists have expanded the economy, the first struggle begins. But in Italy in 1969 there was a huge wave of class struggle in the period of the boom economy, when the working class said: Alright you have huge profits, you propose to me to buy a car in the advertisements, but I have no money, give me more money. And the process of class struggle began. Of course, in Italy there were many questions that opened up along the road after a

long hot autumn at the end of the 1970s. But the process started in the period of boom. There is a period of the development of capitalism, of production, and the class struggle rises.

Put forward crudely – economic crisis equals passivity, boom equals radicalisation or vice versa – it is a one-sided way to approach the issue. It depends on what has gone before: what was, what is, and what will become. Let us take the two examples that Trotsky gives, of the 1905-07 revolution, where there was a revolutionary wave in the first Russian Revolution. The defeat of the revolution then coincided with the downturn in the economy and a worsening of living standards. This did not radicalise the proletariat but disheartened them even more. In the crisis of 1929-33, because the US working class was not prepared, it was stunned. There were no strong trade unions, they were not organised in the new big industries, only a small minority was organised. There were no mass socialist or communist parties. It took four years, and only when the economy began to develop from 1933-36, for three million workers to pour into the trade unions and create new huge, potentially radical and even revolutionary, unions. The possibility of a mass labour party based on the trade unions was posed in America. John L Lewis, the mineworkers' leader, was on the point of launching the idea of a labour party in the late 1930s. These are two examples. It all depends on what has gone before and what will develop.

Take this boom, for instance. Normally in a boom, which is to some extent what we have had in the 1990s, the working class manages to increase its living standards – pushing up wages and achieving shorter working hours. When there is an upswing, in general, the unions should be strengthened. Yet this boom has resulted in a weakening of the working class because of the trade union leaders. The workers' organisations act as a huge brake. We could give many examples of this in Britain as you could for Italy.

It is necessary here to make a general point. In the next period, if a 1929-type collapse takes place, it is possible that the working class could be stunned. This is because neo-liberalism has weakened the trade union movement and lowered consciousness. A 1929 situation, on the industrial front, could further weaken the working class. If you have 600 workers in a workplace and it goes down to 300, the workers who are left would say, I have to keep my head down here. They may conclude that it is not the time to fight. If there is then an increase in the workforce in a small boom then, possibly, they would feel stronger and be prepared to fight in that situation.

However, while on the industrial front the working class was stunned in the US between 1929 and 1933, politically it was a different matter. A layer of politically advanced workers began to draw anti-capitalist, socialist and revolutionary conclusions and some moved towards the Communist Party. The capitalist system was shown to be bankrupt. So to some extent we have to differentiate between the industrial and political responses of the proletariat in a given situation. There will be occasions when a worker will say, I cannot fight industrially, I am too weak, but I can do something politically, I can move in a political direction, I can make a difference in this field. A 1929-type situation is not the best for us in this period, after what has gone before.

If there is a small drop in production in the next period, which undermines the confidence of the bourgeoisie, that would have a radicalising effect without disheartening the working class. Also it would raise political questions about the viability of the system. However, we cannot determine the character of the economic cycle in advance. We have to analyse each situation as it develops. There is no cook book, no recipe which can determine *a priori* exactly how the economic period opening up will be. Perspectives are a rough guide. It is an approximation of the situation, it is not a blueprint, as to the precise economic and political processes that will unfold.

No 'final crisis'

You say that the prediction of Trotsky before the Second World War was right.

In one sense, yes.

Yet, in the *Transitional Programme* he wrote that the productive forces cannot develop any more and that capitalism has no solution. After that you say his prediction was right because you had a revolutionary period in Europe. But his prediction was broader. He was also sure that Stalinism would fall during the Second World War. He was sure that there would be a rising of the working class during or just after the Second World War. The working class would arrive at a revolutionary level, so destroying and defeating Stalinism. Because of their level of consciousness, Russian workers defeated the Mensheviks and the Social Revolutionaries.

But the Bolshevik party had led a revolution before, in 1905, and were much stronger in their roots than any other revolutionary force was in Europe or internationally in 1943-47. They were much stronger and they did not have the added impediment of the Stalinists.

The general prediction of Trotsky was that there were some weaknesses; we can say that capitalism destroyed much of the productive forces. During the Second World War you have not only the destruction of the productive forces, you have inventions, development of the chemical industry, plastics. There was the first nuclear bomb.

It always happens that there are new inventions developed in war. They are a by-product of military conflict.

Today, if you only look at the GDP worldwide you have a development under capitalism...

In the period 1950-75, four times the rate of development of any other time in history.

...But if you look worldwide, you have stagnation, the artificial development of the United States and a rapid development of China, India, etc, can we then continue to speak of the productive forces stagnating as discussed by the Marxists?

Marxism is the science of perspectives but all perspectives are conditional including those dealing with the development of the economy. I will make a general point here. Engels said in the introduction to the *Class Struggles in France*, it is never possible to have a complete view of what is happening in capitalism at each stage, a completely accurate view, especially in a crisis. Only afterwards when the statistics are compiled is it possible to have a complete picture. That is true today even with computers, the latest analyses of the stock exchanges and with all the means of gathering information, because capitalism is still a blind system. It is the blind development of the productive forces behind the backs of society. It is an unplanned system and despite all the attempts of the capitalists to plan it falls down because of private ownership and the nation state, with the individual and national interests of each capitalist taking priority.

The second point is that it would be wrong to use a statement of Trotsky or Lenin in one historical context and say that is the ultimate truth. Let me give an example. Trotsky said in the *Transitional Programme*, within ten years not one stone upon another of the old internationals will be left and the Fourth International will be the biggest force on the planet. Some Trotskyists then claimed, ten years later: "It is now 1947, next year we will be the biggest force on the planet." It was using the letter of Trotsky against the spirit, method of analysis and approach.

Trotsky also wrote that capitalism was stagnating. But if you took capitalism from 1918-38, net production grew. But when we are talking about the productive forces we are also talking about the proletariat as well. This is the most important productive force, and the inability of capitalism to absorb the working class is a symptom of endemic crisis. Apart from 1918-29 in the US, the inter-war period was characterised by short booms and drawn-out crises, which characterised the whole period. From 1918 some countries were in a much better position than others and the world economy was less dominant than it is today. But even then, Trotsky objected when Zinoviev said in 1924 that we were entering the 'final crisis of capitalism'. There is no such thing as a 'final crisis'. Capitalism will always find a way out on the bones of the proletariat, by the destruction of the productive forces. 1929-33 saw the destruction of the productive forces, of constant capital and variable capital, and the inter-war period saw a holding back of technology.

You talked about the use of technology after 1945 but do not forget that, while there was a substantial development of technology *before* the Second World War, it could not be utilised fully because of the crisis. Twenty to 30 years ago British capitalism had two thirds of the research and development of the whole of Europe. But it could not fully use its ingenuity and technological edge in its domestic market, which was too small. Its invention could only be properly utilised by bigger powers. To return to Trotsky. He said unless the proletariat takes power then, through the destruction of the workers' organisations and drastically reduced living standards or through war, capitalism will find a new equilibrium. There is no 'final crisis of capitalism' unless the working class takes power. It will only be resolved by the conscious action of the proletariat to change society. Then, of course, there will be opportunities to develop technology fully.

Trotsky was right in his prediction of a post-war revolutionary wave. What you said about the Soviet Union is true: he expected Stalinism to collapse. But he later made a correction in his unfinished biography *Stalin*. He wrote that capitalism worldwide was in such a parlous state that there was an international tendency towards collectivisation and therefore it was even possible that the Russian Stalinist regime could go on longer. He was correct in anticipating the revolutionary wave. What he could not estimate – and nobody could have done this before the war – was the ability of social democracy and Stalinism together to successfully betray this revolutionary wave. The two powers which emerged from the Second World War strengthened were the US on the one side and Russian Stalinism on the other. The latter extended its power to Eastern Europe and rapidly rebuilt the Soviet Union. That could not have been anticipated. The destruction of the war laid the basis, together with the political factors, for the economic recovery. Without the political factors, Europe would have remained broken-backed after 1945.

So radicalised was Europe by the devastating effects of the war that the German social democracy's slogan of 1948 was for a 'socialist united states of Europe'! Italy was convulsed in that whole period, France too. The stability came really after 1950, and came very slowly. So the political preconditions for this framework of capitalist growth were absolutely essential.

In Trotsky's writings are some of the keys to understanding the world today. But to use a key successfully, you have to know how to put it in the lock and how to turn it. They are not a philosopher's stone. By merely repeating the words of Trotsky in a much more complicated world situation we will not advance one iota. That is, unfortunately, what some of the 'Trotskyists' have done. They have repeated the phrases of Trotsky on a whole number of issues without understanding the context, and without understanding the historical background and the changes that have taken place today.

Trotsky posed a whole number of questions, such as the idea of a black republic in South Africa and a separate state in the South of the US for blacks. But events worked out differently. On the Jewish question, look at Trotsky's position and the way events actually developed. One has to have an ability to analyse new phenomena by trying to utilise and understand the method of Trotsky but not just by repeating by rote the phraseology of Trotsky.

The environment and China

I asked a question about the new approach, the question of the productive forces, because the Marxist movement says there are developments in the level of productive forces and socialism is possible. So we have two questions: worldwide, the productive forces are so big that you could have socialism tomorrow, I think you agree.

Yes, because we can abolish scarcity.

There are the possibilities for planning the economy...

For the first time in history, want, privation, poverty and unemployment could disappear, in one generation.

This is the first question. The second question is the kind of development of the productive forces under capitalism. One simple example. It is impossible, unlike Italy where every two people has a car, use a car, that the Chinese and Indian people could have the same. It is not just an economic question, there is oil...

It is environmental as well.

All the things bought in Western countries, the poor people cannot buy. It is not only economic but environmental. Did Trotsky ever speak about the question of the environment? Is there a new relationship in the development of the productive forces and the world, or not?

This is a very important issue and is crucial, especially for the new generation and for the whole of humankind. But it is not true that Marx, Engels Lenin and Trotsky never spoke about the environment, they did. In the third volume of *Capital*, Marx makes the point: "From the standpoint of a higher economic form of society, private ownership of the globe by single individuals will appear quite as absurd as private ownership of one man by another. Even a whole society, a nation, or even all simultaneously existing societies taken together, are not owners of the globe. They are only its possessors… they must hand it down to succeeding generations in an improved condition." We must pass the world on to the next generation in a better state than we found it. Trotsky spoke in a similar vein in works like *Radio, Science and Technique*. The Bolsheviks were very interested in the harmonisation between the productive forces and the environment.

We face an unprecedented situation today. The kind of development of the productive forces under capitalism in an unplanned way, even if you do not have a new economic crisis, means that the majority of humankind will have to challenge this system on the question of the environment alone in order to prevent an unstoppable decline. The leading Chinese environmentalist, semi-officially supported by the government, has said that for China to reach the living standards of the US will need the resources of four worlds! Do we conclude from this that the Chinese people will never reach the living standards of the American people today and that they are condemned forever to backwardness? I think it would be wrong to say this. We can have sustainable growth and we can avoid the crimes that have been committed against the environment by capitalism and Stalinism.

Let us just take the question of China and India or the neo-colonial world as a whole. Under capitalism, industry equals high living standards and wealth while agriculture, in general, equals cultural backwardness and poverty. In order to overcome that problem on the basis of capitalism, the backward, economically underdeveloped countries have to try and imitate the advanced industrial countries in every respect by developing their own steel, car and all the other modern industries. There is a huge duplication accompanied by massive urbanisation. For the first time in history, just over 50% of the world's population live in urban areas.

This itself will create massive urban conurbations of 20, 30, 40 millions, in the future. To avoid this nightmare poses the need for democratic planning. It raises the necessity for a new world division of labour.

Under a world socialist plan, for instance, agriculture would not equal backwardness, and industry would not automatically equal higher living standards. The surplus that would be generated by industry and by agriculture to a degree would be developed through a world plan. On this basis it would be possible to harmonise the resources of the world between industry and the agricultural areas to the mutual benefit of the peoples of the world. It is not for us to work it out in detail how the working class and the poor will do this when they take power. The Stalinists attempted in a bureaucratic fashion to organise a division of labour in Eastern Europe. They had grain countries like Romania and those like Bulgaria for fruit. Others concentrated on different branches of production. But it was done in a bureaucratic fashion and the agricultural areas remained the most backward. Their wealth was sucked out for the benefit of the bureaucracy in the industrialised urban areas.

We are opposed to nuclear power, nuclear fission, but the possibility of clean energy and the resources to be put into that have been outlined in a pamphlet produced by one of our comrades. [*Planning Green Growth*, by Pete Dickenson.] This poses the need for socialist planning of industry, society and the environment, which goes into some of these issues. The environment is absolutely crucial. It is not just an abstract question. Our comrades in places like Pakistan, Nigeria, Sri Lanka, in Malaysia, which I visited, have to fight environmental battles in their societies to a much greater extent than existed in the past. When I was in Malaysia in 2005, there was one Chinese village I was taken to by the Socialist Party of Malaysia (PSM), which is not affiliated to the CWI but with whom we have friendly relations. There was a rubber factory poisoning the people in the village and, as a result of a mass campaign, they got the rubber factory removed. So the environment is both a general and also a concrete question.

I would add that Marx in the first volume of *Capital*, in the chapter on the working day, also provides a number of examples of the adulteration of food like bread – which is even the case today – and of the effect of capitalism on the environment. It is not true, as some of the environmentalists like to say, that Marx was only interested in a one-sided way in the development of the productive forces and the economic aspect. He was concerned about the alienation, which is a major problem today, the adulteration of food, the question of the environment, the need for each generation to leave the world in a better state for the next generation.

The falling rate of profit

What do you think of Marx's theory of the falling rate of profit? Marx wrote about it as a tendency and also about a counter-tendency.

We think that Marx was correct about the tendency of the rate of profit to decline. Historically, there has been a colossal growth of constant capital, dead labour if you like, to use Marx's terminology, compared to living labour, variable capital. Consequently, capital, said Marx, has a tendency to become less and less 'organic', with a tendency to create relatively smaller and smaller annual increments. However, the capitalists express that as the technical growth of capitalism but dead labour predominates over living labour. It is generally accepted even by pre-Marxist economists as an empirical fact that, as capitalism grew, the rate of profit declined. Marx described it as a 'tendency' and analysed this wonderfully in detail in part three of the third volume of *Capital*.

What immediately concerns the capitalists is not the tendency of the rate of profit to decline or even the rate of profit. It is the amount of profit which they can accumulate. The 'counteracting causes' are things like the depression of wages below their value, which is what we have seen to some extent in the 1990s with neoliberal measures. Profits for the capitalists are at an unprecedented level, the highest they have been for 70 years in the case of the US. But it is also a general phenomenon throughout the advanced industrial countries. There are a number of other counteracting factors which can have an effect but again, to use Marx's terminology, there are certain 'impassable limits' beyond which the capitalists cannot go.

There is empirical evidence to show that Marx was right but this process is revealed over time and sometimes over long historical periods. We do not talk here necessarily of two, three or five years. It is a long-term trend. But periods can be reached where there is a sudden collapse in profits. In Britain, for instance, in one year of the 1970s, there was an absolute drop in the mass of profits. There is a constant battle between the classes to garner the surplus created by the working class, thereby controlling art, science, culture and therefore the state. When the amount of profit drops absolutely, even the capitalists stop investing. Why should they invest £2million when they only get £1,975,000 back? When they refuse to invest, then there can then be a crisis. This results in a 'jamming' of the system leading to the crisis itself. Unlike some people who claim to be Marxists and who dispute this aspect of Marxism, we do not. We think the tendency of the rate of profit to decline is correct theoretically and it can be verified empirically, especially today.

The Middle East

What is your general analysis and judgement about the Middle East, about the war in Lebanon and its end with the UN resolution on the use of the French and Italian troops?

The third invasion of Lebanon arose over the kidnapping of Israeli soldiers but that, in turn, was really a solidarity action of Hezbollah with the Palestinians, who face terrible persecution. Gaza is one giant prison camp. The economic situation in the Palestinian areas is unprecedented. Never in its history, even going back to the 1930s, has there been so much poverty, unemployment, suffering and desperation as there is now. Hezbollah started this action partly in solidarity with the Palestinian people. Israel has arrested and imprisoned 9,000 Palestinians. Also, Hezbollah fighters are in Israeli prisons. This action was used by Israel as a pretext for a preconceived plan to attack Lebanon and Hezbollah. The promise of the Israeli government of Olmert that the infrastructure of Lebanon would be thrown back 20 years has been partly realised in the colossal destruction inflicted by Israel.

However, this is the first time since the formation of the state of Israel that the Israeli ruling class and the Israel Defence Force (IDF) have faced such an open defeat on the field of battle. The IDF only got a couple of miles into Lebanon. It was confronted by determined resistance and was not able to overcome Hezbollah, signifying a defeat for the Israeli ruling class in general. It is also a defeat for US imperialism and its policies in relation to Lebanon because they had initiated a series of offensive actions up to the invasion, including the eviction of Syria from Lebanon. It was also a step towards further attacks on Syria. There was also speculation that the war in Lebanon was preparation for further military action against Iran, although that is a different question. We support the withdrawal of all foreign troops from Lebanon. The Lebanese people should have the right to decide their own fate.

The consequences of the war have been profound on both sides. First of all, Hezbollah, based upon the poor Shia masses, has a history which is somewhat different to other groups which have Islamic antecedents. It is different from Hamas, for instance, at the present time. There are some similarities in the sense that Hezbollah and Hamas are products of the Israeli ruling class's aggression and attacks on Lebanon and the Palestinians. Hezbollah was created as a result of the Israeli intervention of 1982 and was actually formed in the Iranian embassy in Damascus. However, it would be wrong for us to conclude from this that Hezbollah is just a stooge of the Iranian regime. Of course, it has connections because of the Shia links but it is not just a 'creature' of Tehran. It has developed independently.

Members of the Lebanese Communist Party, for instance, and others on the left whose independent influence had declined came in behind Hezbollah as a resistance organisation. There have even been favourable statements recently from Nasrullah, the leader of Hezbollah, about the role of Che Guevara, of socialists, in combating imperialism. So it is not a typical Islamic organisation. In fact, it has been forced to drop the idea of an Islamic state in Lebanon as a result of the pressure it has come under and the support it received from groups other than the Shias, such as the Sunnis, Christians and so on.

In the course of the war, Hezbollah played, at least partially, the role of a legitimate organisation of Lebanese national resistance to imperialist intervention. This does not mean to say we give uncritical support to Hezbollah. It is not a socialist organi-sation. But in the war and afterwards its leadership was aware of the potential for increasing its support amongst the non-Shia sections of the population. Nasrullah welcomed the initial support of 80% of the Christians, Druze and other confession-al groups in Lebanon. This has created a new situation within Lebanon. But unless Hezbollah develops in a class direction and puts forward a class and socialist alternative its development could be stalled. It has received widespread popularity by giving grants of $12,000 to those whose houses have been destroyed. Signs with 'Made in America' on bombed houses directly connect the bombing to US imperi-alism, a reflection in any case of the consciousness of the Lebanese population. Inevitably under capitalism, where there is a struggle for resources, the leaders of the different ethnic and religious groups will attempt to exploit the position for themselves, therefore temporary unity can break down. However, out of this present situation may come a new class consciousness. There were movements of workers on electricity prices before the war began; a class movement from below was developing in Lebanon. The role of socialists, Marxists and Trotskyists is to support legitimate actions of resistance of oppressed people against imperialist intervention but at the same time to raise the socialist and class issues.

We have made general points on the UN in our publications. It is no different in the modern era to the League of Nations, which Lenin and Trotsky opposed. We have to recognise that there is a feeling amongst many workers that, after the terrible experience of the Lebanese people, maybe a 'buffer' is needed between the belliger-ents to prevent a new outbreak of war. But it was very striking that there was no suggestion of the UN going in by Blair or Bush until the Israelis had bombed the hell out of Lebanon and were in the process of trying to realise their 'war aims'. Blair did not even call for a ceasefire, which led to mass revulsion in Britain and probably was the tipping point in the clamour for his removal. He will be removed from office in any case in the next period. There was general disgust that he was not even prepared to call for a ceasefire when women and children were being killed and injured, when collective punishment was being inflicted on the people of Lebanon. The UN as a solution was rejected by the Lebanese people. UNIFIL had a presence in Lebanon before the war began in the so-called buffer zone. They did nothing to prevent the war. The UN could only be wheeled in once the combatants themselves had agreed that the war would not go any further at that stage.

Will the UN maintain the peace? No. Why should an ordinary worker in Britain or Italy, who would never think of turning to the employers to solve his or her problems, embrace the employers' organisations internationally, like the UN, which is ultimately in the grip of US imperialism? In fact a recent article in the *Financial Times* appealed to the US, which finances the UN, to support it because it is "good for US business", which is true. US imperialism will use the UN when it serves them, when it is acting on behalf of the so-called 'international community' as was the case in the Korean War. It will go outside the UN, as in the Vietnam War, when it cannot necessarily get support. Over Iraq, when it faced difficulties in the UN, it resorted to the 'coalition of the willing', which is now the 'coalition of the reluctant and very unwilling'. The UN is not an alternative. We say the real solution or 'buffer force' in Lebanon is the Lebanese working class coming together with the Israeli working class to oppose the war because they are the people who suffer. In Israel, the Olmert government will collapse. In all probability it will be replaced be a more right-wing government, maybe led by Netanyahu. Another war is rooted in the situation, and it will be the ordinary Lebanese and Israeli people who will suffer. In that sense, the UN and its resolution, ratifying the deployment of French and Italian troops under the blue helmets and banner of the UN, are not the solutions to the problems of Lebanon. It is the working class in Israel, in Lebanon and throughout the Middle East as a whole, with the support of the working class in Europe and elsewhere, which holds the key to the situation.

Hezbollah

The second question is that you say you support the right of Hezbollah and the Lebanese people to resist but you criticise the use of the Katyusha rockets against Israeli towns. Some people could answer that there was such different strength of forces in this war that Hezbollah used what was possible – they had very intelligent rockets to attack government buildings and not Israeli towns. How can we decide on military tactics of organisations that concretely defend their own citizens in Lebanon?

First of all, we have to make it clear that Hezbollah and any other Lebanese national resistance forces have the right to militarily resist Israeli intervention. That goes without saying. It has the right to confront the IDF, to use rockets to attack Israeli military targets and bring down military aeroplanes. That is a legitimate part of a military resistance. Hezbollah and the Lebanese resistance in a war also have the right to attack specific military targets within Israel itself.

As far as military tactics are concerned, there were mistakes made by both sides which rebounded on them. After the kidnapping of Israeli troops, the Israeli government concluded that by targeting civilians, not necessarily Hezbollah, the suffering of the Lebanese would result in the alienation of Hezbollah from the population. The bombing would drive a wedge between Hezbollah and the Lebanese population. Exactly the opposite took place. The Lebanese population, rather than blaming Hezbollah, indicted the Israeli state and began to support Hezbollah as a legitimate representative of national resistance.

On the other hand, American correspondent Charles Glass, who was kidnapped by Hezbollah in the 1980s and is an informed writer on the Middle East and Vietnam, in an interview in the *London Review of Books*, made the point that Nasrullah probably also thought from his point of view that the 4,000 rockets fired by Hezbollah would produce a schism between the Israeli government and the Israeli working class. But it did not happen. The situation in Israel was a mirror image of what took place in Lebanon. The Israeli population more than in other wars in the first instance came behind the government – 90% support.

The second issue is the rockets that landed in Israeli Arab areas. They did not just target Israeli Jews (that is impossible) and even that would be wrong, but they struck Israeli Arabs. In the most mixed town in Israel, Haifa, the Israeli Arabs were seriously affected. There was a mass exodus from Haifa. In the aftermath of the war, some of the Israeli Arabs said: well, some of us were injured or died but that is part of the war. But in general, that is not the attitude. Quite apart from the Israeli Arabs, it drove the Israeli working class into the arms of their own ruling class. It was counterproductive just as terrorism in general is. We would not dispute Hezbollah's right to resist but on that particular tactic we think they were wrong. It was indiscriminate and therefore wrong in that concrete situation.

The consequences in the rest of the Arab world are another matter. The Lebanese war has had a ripple effect throughout the Middle East. Originally, the feudal, semi-feudal and capitalist rulers of Egypt and Saudi Arabia came out and attacked Hezbollah for allegedly provoking this war. This was mostly because they are Sunni, and Hezbollah was originally Shia and its main base still is. But this created a split between the ruling classes of the Middle East and the Arab 'street'. The overwhelming majority of the Arab masses reasoned: how is it that a guerrilla force estimated at no more than 3,000 to 5,000 fighters has humbled the mighty Israeli military machine. Yet all the Arab armies with all the gold of the Gulf States, with all the potential power of Egypt and the others, could not have the same effect? It is the first time since 1948 that the Israeli military machine has been stopped in its tracks.

Israel and Palestine

In Italy, the far left has always had a not very good approach about the position 'two peoples, two states'. Firstly, because the normal position, not only on the left but in general, is that the Palestinians need their own state. There is a big difference between anti-Semitism and anti-Zionism, and in Italy there is an ideological attack against anti-Semitism. In the international revolutionary movement and also in the Fourth International after the Second World War when there was partition, the Fourth International was against it. There was a section in Palestine that voted against partition and was for one country with minority rights. So we have always supported the position of one state with rights for the minority in Palestine. We are Marxists and we believe that in a future world there will be no borders. The two states solution means not less but more states. Of course there is an important working class in Israel but the most important is in Egypt, so the question is: should socialists today support 'two peoples two states' and how do you reply to those who put forward a one-state solution?

The most important law of the dialectic is that truth is concrete. On the historical issues, it is indisputable that Trotskyism, starting from Trotsky himself, opposed a Jewish state being formed on the territory of Palestine. That was his general position in the inter-war period. However, he modified his stance after the Nazis' persecution of the Jews became evident. A new situation had emerged. Trotsky was always flexible when taking account of new important factors. There was a feeling on the part of the Jewish population to get out of Germany and Europe and with this went increased support for the dream of a new homeland.

Under socialism, reasoned Trotsky, if the Jews wanted a state in, say, a part of Africa, with the agreement of the African people, or in Latin America, it could be considered but not in Palestine. Here, it would be a bloody trap for the Jews. It is amazing how this prediction has been borne out. There was an article in the *Financial Times* recently, on the Middle East, in which some bourgeois professor said: the most dangerous place for any Jew in the world today is in Israel. It is the bloody trap which Trotsky warned against. The Trotskyist movement opposed the establishment of a separate Jewish state in Israel because it was a wedge against the Arab revolution. Israel was set up as a result of the colonisation of Arab lands, by driving out the Palestinians and by using a mixture of radical and even 'socialistic', nationalist rhetoric directed towards a Jewish population who had escaped the nightmare of the Holocaust and the Second World War.

A state or a series of states can be established by the brutal displacement of peoples. Look at the removal of the Greek population from many parts of Asia Minor and of Turks from Greece following the collapse of the Ottoman Empire. If you went back and redrew the map, you would now have huge exchanges of populations. As a result of a terrible crime against the Jews in Europe under Nazism-capitalism, this was then used as justification for a crime against the Palestinian people. That remains an indisputable historical fact.

Two states?

However, the reality now is that, in the course of time, a Jewish or Israeli national consciousness has been created. What do Marxists say to this? Just ignore the real situation and continue with the old position? The solution of the USFI, the Socialist Workers' Party (SWP) and others on the left is a Palestinian state – which was originally our policy – of a unified Palestinian state with autonomous rights for the Jews. They put it forward in a bourgeois context. We always put it forward in a socialist framework. We do not have the position of a two-state solution on a bourgeois basis as do, for instance, some tiny groups. That is a utopian dream. If the Oslo accords gave only a small portion of historic Palestine to the Palestinian people, under Olmert's proposals for a redivision of Palestine, which is now off the agenda, it would leave just 10% as a state for the Palestinians. It is a Bantustan. It is not a viable state as far as the Palestinians are concerned. There is no possibility of a viable capitalist two-state solution. An interim arrangement could not be ruled out but it is not a solution to the national problems of either the Palestinians or the Israelis. Nevertheless, the idea of a two-state solution, of a socialist Palestine and a socialist Israel within a socialist confederation of the Middle East is, in our opinion, a correct programmatic demand.

The question we have to ask ourselves is how are the legitimate aspirations of both societies to be met? In both populations there is now a national consciousness, irrespective of what has happened in the past. This is our starting point. Before the

Lebanese war, the idea began to develop within the Palestinians that they were condemned to remain within some kind of 'Greater Israel'. Some Palestinians then said: we want the vote, and this frightened the Israeli ruling class. They were concerned about a demographic time bomb which would change the character of the Israeli state. That is why Sharon and then Olmert decided they could not maintain the Greater Israel perspective – from the Mediterranean to the Dead Sea and incorporating Gaza – for one very simple reason. If the Palestinians were kept imprisoned in that state, they would then demand equal rights: the right to vote, one person one vote, as in South Africa under apartheid. Within a measurable period of time they could become the majority within Israel. So the dream of Likud of a Greater Israel had to be abandoned and Sharon and Olmert went over to the idea of repartition, which would give them a Jewish majority in an Israeli state and a truncated bourgeois state in what was left of Palestine. This was acquiesced to by the Bush regime.

We have to face the fact that the Palestinian and Jewish peoples have decided that they could not live together in one state. That is their consciousness. What does a Marxist and a Trotskyist say in this situation? You say that we do not want further states, we do not want the break up of unified states and, abstractly, that is true. But socialists and Marxists cannot compel different peoples to live in the same state. There is still a national question in the background in Italy, in Alto Adige. Who knows? That could come up in the future. That is like a shadow, which in some circumstances could take on substance. What would be our position? We may have to accept it. It is possible that Spain could break up. It is possible that India could break up. India is not a unified state in many senses. It was unified in one sense for the first time by British imperialism but it is now made up of different 'nationalities'. Lenin said we cannot build a new socialist, communist society on the basis of the slightest compulsion against a nationality, a group or a layer in society. Look at the lengths to which the Bolsheviks were prepared to go in order to convince opponents of their ideas by argument and example. They were even prepared, after the revolution, to say to the anarchists: well, we disagree with your proposal for 'no state' but we will consider giving you a certain part of Russia. You can establish an anarchist commune there. Then let us go through this experiment with you, which will convince you that your alternative of an anarchist 'stateless' society in the transition between capitalism and socialism would be seen to be utopian. The civil war and all its consequences meant that this idea was not carried out but the approach was valid. Lenin and Trotsky understood that the national question is similar to the land question. Giving small parcels of land to the peasants may represent a step backwards economically but they had no alternative in Russia in 1917 if they were to win the peasants. It is a case of one step back with the hope of two steps forward in the future.

If you had a two-state socialist alternative, the Israeli masses could approach the Palestinian masses and discuss with them: 'We think this could be a solution', or vice versa. A dialogue and discussion could be opened up. Approach the Israeli workers with the idea that they would be forcibly incorporated into a common state with Palestinians against their will and they will say: 'We will fight to the death. We have nowhere else to go.'

This is not the situation of South Africa under apartheid. George Galloway, the Respect MP in London, has raised the idea that there could be a "de Klerk moment" in Israel. De Klerk represented the Afrikaners but he decided that the game was up; the whites had to hand over power, or the illusion of power, to the Africans. But that was only possible against the background of the collapse of Stalinism and also on the basis of the bourgeoisification of the African National Congress (ANC). The demographic relationship in South Africa in 1990 was seven non-whites to every white. That is not the situation in Israel-Palestine at this stage. The Israeli population will fight. Even the 'peace camp' will fight if their right to a separate state is under threat. The Israeli working class will fight if you threaten them that they will be driven into the sea. Therefore, transitional demands are necessary in order to approach the masses. We say: you decide what the borders of a future state will be under a social-ist confederation. It is even possible, on the basis of a socialist revolution in the Middle East, that the Israelis and the Palestinians would then decide to live together in one state with autonomy for both. We cannot say beforehand. But the dialectic of the situation is if you try and impose one state on them now, it will be rejected.

Israel is a running sore in the region. A key question in the Middle Eastern revolu-tion is how to split the Israeli workers away from the ruling class. Challenge them, threaten the idea of an Israeli 'homeland', then there is no chance of achieving this. The Israeli state is a creation of imperialism. But an indigenous arms industry has developed, technical industries, etc, and they can hold the Arab population at bay almost indefinitely, or as long as capitalism survives. What hope is there for the Palestinian masses on the basis of this situation? There is no alternative on a capital-ist basis. A two-state capitalist solution is no solution at all. It will result in an abortion of a state. A two-state socialist solution, the borders of which we cannot define in advance but which would be voluntarily and democratically defined by the Palestinian and Israeli people, is a very important weapon for approaching these workers. We accept that many Arab workers, to begin with, will have the attitude that the Israeli state has to be dismantled. It is an imperialist wedge against the Arab revolution. But once it is posed correctly, it can be accepted. It is noticeable that, before the current war, the population in Palestine had reluctantly concluded that a two-state solution was the alternative and the Israeli population had come to the same conclusion. But now, if it means a new border, with only 10% of historic Palestine in a new 'state', that is a different situation.

On the national question, Lenin's writings are amongst the treasures of humanity, as Trotsky put it. But the national question today is immeasurably more complicated. For Marxists, it has two sides. We are opposed to bourgeois nationalism, which seeks to divide the working class. We are for the maximum unity of the working class across borders, continents and worldwide but at the same time we oppose the forcible incorporation of distinct nationalities into one state against their will. We would support, for instance, the people of Quebec if they voted by a majority in a referendum to separate from Canada. We are also in favour of an independent socialist Scotland. But if, in Canada, the Quebec bourgeois then refuse to accept the rights of the minorities within an independent Quebec, we would oppose them. Some of the Quebec nationalists are for the independence of Quebec but are against the rights of the native peoples. We oppose that.

Joe Higgins - Socialist Party Member in the Irish parliament

Ireland and the National Question

What about the example of Ireland? There is the situation where 26 counties are in one state following the compromise of the 1920s and six are in Northern Ireland. Only in two are the Protestants a majority.

No, in Northern Ireland there are six counties and in 1969 two thirds of the population in those six counties were Protestant and one third Catholic. The demographic pattern has changed today but the Protestants are still in a majority.

You have the situation that the revolutionary movement always supports a 32-county state...

Marx and Engels did, yes. Trotsky and Lenin, yes.

You have the imperialism of Great Britain, which separated one part of the country from the rest, split on religious grounds. We know the situation. But does the working class and socialist movement in the South support a unified country where the Protestant minority can live? Because this division is artificial historically.

That cannot be said now. That position had some validity prior to the partition of 1921. Ireland was a colony of British imperialism up to 1921. After partition, 26 counties formed the Irish 'Free' State. The six counties in the North were left behind – a population one third Catholic, two thirds Protestant. It was an artificial creation. But in the consciousness of the majority of the population – the Protestants – it has become more than that. It is a separate state linked to Britain which has existed since 1921, for 85 years now. The Protestant population's consciousness is that they will not be coerced into a united Ireland. Southern Ireland has been dominated historically by the Catholic Church, with no divorce, no contraception, democratic rights severely curtailed historically (it is different now). Protestants will not go into a state where they will be a discriminated-against minority. They wish to maintain 'British democratic rights' which, ironically, were severely curtailed by Thatcher and now by Blair. But that is their consciousness, not just the petty-bourgeoisie but the working class too.

The minority Catholic population, the bulk of whom has never been reconciled to that state, has been discriminated against. The CWI has a very good organisation in Northern Ireland which has fought to create class unity between Catholic and Protestant workers. In 1969 I was in Northern Ireland, in Derry and in Belfast, and we won over Catholic and Protestant workers and youth. Ted Grant and I spoke at a meeting of about 300 young people in 1970 in Derry city. We went into the Bogside in that city and in Belfast with armed gunmen and met the IRA. We always disagreed with them. We said that you are pursuing a terrorist campaign, a guerrilla struggle in an urban area, not in the traditional rural areas, and it cannot succeed. This is not like Vietnam, where a majority of the peasant population supported the guerrilla struggle. It is not even like Algeria, where the FLN in the Algerian war of 1956-62 fought as a national resistance to which we gave support, including practical help, against French imperialism. The 'colons' who supported the French there were only 10% of the population and they were driven out. A guerrilla struggle, as with the IRA's 30-year campaign in Northern Ireland, based upon a minority of the population could not succeed.

The dialectic, the paradox, is that by 1969, the British bourgeoisie would have accepted a united Ireland. The political, military and strategic factors – which led it to divide Ireland in 1921 – had evaporated. With the disappearance of the British 'Empire' and with the collapse of the world role of its military, particularly its naval prowess, the naval bases in Ireland were no longer vital for the British ruling class. A united Ireland would have been cheaper for Britain. But they had helped to foster the Protestant population's opposition to a capitalist united Ireland. They were implacably opposed – and still are - to going into a united Ireland and they will fight to avoid this. In answer to the IRA's campaign of terrorism, directed against the British state, we said your campaign cannot succeed. Mao's famous aphorism was that the guerrilla is a fish that swims in water, you must have favourable and sufficient water in which the fish can swim and be successful. But a minority will not coerce the majority. The IRA's answer was: 'we have a majority of the population of the 26 counties supporting us.' But the situation had moved on since 1921.

We were for the withdrawal of British troops but it is necessary to put an alternative in their place. If the British had withdrawn their troops from Northern Ireland, it would have been a bit like Lebanon, a civil war would have broken out unless there was a class alternative. In that civil war, you would not be dealing with a population which was unprepared to fight. The Protestants were armed. In such a civil war, Catholics could be driven out of parts of the North and Protestants from other parts. There would be a repartition of the North. The repercussions of this would be a nightmare, not just in Ireland but in England, Wales and Scotland too, which could be flooded with refugees.

As opposed to the sectarians on both sides of the religious divide, we launched the idea of a united struggle of the working class including a trade union defence force, linking Catholics and Protestants together. The main meeting point of Catholics and Protestants was in the factories. So we put forward this demand in order to try and cement class unity.

The IRA conducted a 30-year campaign. The SWP in Britain, the USFI, the Morenoites in Latin America, because they did not understand the national question and its reflection in Northern Ireland, usually gave uncritical support to the Republicans, to the IRA. The Good Friday agreement between the leaders of the Republican movement and a section of the Unionists, presided over by the British and Irish governments, was, in effect, an admission by the IRA of what we had said. They could not win this military struggle and so they ended the war. 'The war was over', they declared. They did not win the war, they did not drive British imperialism out. They tried to rationalise it for their own supporters by saying: we have 'legitimacy', we have become a political force and party and, in the course of time, we will become the majority in Northern Ireland as a whole. That might happen in time but the Protestant population would still not go into a united capitalist Ireland. A united socialist Ireland which would be no threat to them would be an entirely different proposition.

Even then, all sides, and particularly the Protestant population, would have to be convinced of this. And that can only be achieved by a united working class in Northern Ireland linked to the workers' movement in Britain and in the South. The forces of the CWI, both in Northern Ireland and in the South, have been the only socialist organisations which have had a consistent and principled position on this issue. We are very proud of them.

Germany

But look at the situation in Germany. There was one nation but politically divided, East and West, which separated families. During the Cold War, the German people, in general, wanted reunification. During the Cold War, perhaps the people thought it would take 200 years!

We supported reunification but on a socialist and class basis.

When in 1961 the Berlin Wall was built and the situation was closed, there was an economic contradiction because workers in the East wanted to go and live in the West. They knew the workers in the West were better off than them; the standard of life was ten times better than in Romania. There is one

**language, one culture, tradition, family connections, it was an intolerable
separation and I think it was similar in Ireland.**

The German people wanted to be united. There was nothing in their consciousness, as a general idea, to prevent it. That is not the situation in Northern
Ireland. The Protestants do not want to go into a united Ireland, we would say into
a *capitalist* united Ireland. There are one and a half million Protestant people who
are still the majority in the North. Are they going to be coerced into a united Ireland?
Are they going to be forced to do this?

The Liga Internacional de los Trabajadores (LIT – International Workers' League) in
Latin America, the Morenoites, have this ridiculous theory. They maintain that there
are a series of imperialist 'enclaves': Israel is an imperialist enclave; Northern
Ireland is an imperialist enclave, etc. These enclaves must be forced into more
unified states. That is not a policy for Marxism to take into the mass movement. It
may sound 'neat' in a small room of sectarians but it is not a policy for going out to
confront the real consciousness of working-class people in a specific situation.
Concrete questions cannot be replied to in an abstract way especially today and
particularly on the national question. It is more complicated than even at the time
of Lenin and Trotsky, and they began to solve only some of the problems. Look at
the way the national question has come back in the former 'Soviet Union' with a
vengeance because of the mishandling of the national question by Stalinism.

The way this question is approached is not one of territory alone or of culture. It is
also a question of consciousness. In the last couple of days, a scientific study has
been published which shows that the DNA of all the inhabitants of Britain and
Ireland comes from Spanish fishermen 6,000 years ago. It seems that the Celts are
not 'ethnically' different from the English from a DNA point of view. But it would be
silly to conclude from this that the whole of the population of Britain and Ireland are
the same because they have the same DNA. From cultural, national and psychological angles, they consider themselves 'British' – English, Scottish, Welsh – or Irish.
That consciousness may dissolve in a future communist society but, between now
and that society, there must be no compulsion or enforcement of people to live in
states that they do not support. The example you gave of Germany is good. Before
1989, there was a German national consciousness although there were different
attitudes in the East and the West. There was a general feeling that 'we are all
German and we want to live together'. It is a bit like the Hungarian people in
Romania. In ideal circumstances they would like to be part of Hungary because they
are discriminated against in Romania. There is a patchwork of nationalities in
Central and Eastern Europe, but the Protestant population of Northern Ireland do

not consider themselves to be the same as the population in the South. How do you deal with that?

Bob Labi: "Things change. Germany has moved on. For instance, when Austria was formed after the First World War, the Austrians did not want to form Austria, they wanted to go into Germany. The first name of Austria was actually 'German Austria'. They were not allowed to join Germany by the victorious powers. Every political party in Austria in the 1920s and 1930s had in its programme some form of unification. The Communist Party stood for a 'Soviet Greater Germany'. It was part of their programme. It was part of the consciousness of Austrian nationality; if you look at the 1920s population breakdown, it was described as German. But consciousness changed, for different reasons. After the Second World War, the idea of unification with Germany was completely off the agenda. At this moment, Austrians see themselves as Austrian not German. Nobody in Austria, not even the far right, except a few sections, has a different attitude. Even Haider, when he became a big force, started stressing Austrian nationalism. He used to be a 'pan-German' then he realised there was a limit on that and he became an Austrian nationalist. It is a question of how consciousness changes.

"It could be said that Ireland 200 or more years ago was not so divided. The impact of the French Revolution in Ireland was bigger amongst the Protestants than the Catholics. They led the rebellion. Partly because of that, British imperialism conciously went for divide-and-rule tactics in Northern Ireland, basing themselves largely amongst the Protestant population. This is the factor we have to take into account now because the situation is always moving on, it is not fixed for all time. This is the consciousness, as has been said, that we are actually dealing with in Northern Ireland."

If in 1918, when the struggle against the British was under way, the Irish labour movement and trade unions had taken an independent class position, they may have been able to win over the Protestant workers of the North. Or if James Connolly had not engaged in the 1916 uprising and been killed, it is possible history would have taken a different turn and we could have seen a united movement. It is not set in stone. But history turned out differently with the creation of two states, first of all 'artificial creations'. But they are not 'enclaves' any more. The Protestant population of Northern Ireland considers they are part of a separate state. The Catholic population felt discriminated against and we had to fight against that discrimination. If the Protestant population of the North said, in a referendum, we want to go into the South, we would support that, including possible autonomous rights for them if they so wish. But it is not on the cards. The only way that the obstacles in their consciousness to entering a united Ireland can be removed is on a class, socialist basis. Also, it is necessary to remove any element of compulsion, that they will be forced into such a state. The only way that can be done is by a united class movement of Catholics and Protestants overcoming their divisions and prejudices.

Iraq and the resistance

In Iraq there is a very complicated situation because of the occupation of the country, mainly by the US and Britain. There are big problems within the 'coalition'. There are big ethnic and religious divisions but also political divisions. The Ba'ath party had roots in the Sunni peoples but it was not a religious party, it was completely secular, and is playing a major role in the resistance. The Shi'ite parties are in government but they do not want the occupation to continue. It is a very complex situation. There is some sort of guerrilla resistance. There are sometimes also class struggles but many clashes between Sunni and Shias. So there is the struggle against occupation and a struggle between the different ethnic and religious groups. In your propaganda material you never, unlike the SWP, say you support the 'resistance', critically or otherwise.

No, we have said we support the resistance of the Iraqi people against the occupation but we cannot give *carte blanche* support to all actions and organisations claiming to lead the 'resistance' because of the situation. To describe the situation in Iraq as turmoil is an understatement. In the British press today, they make the point that the level of torture is now worse than it was under Saddam Hussein. The title of the book *Republic of Fear* can now be applied to the current situation in Iraq, in the torture chambers of the occupiers but also in those of the government. It is an absolute catastrophe. It is a situation that could have been predicted and was predicted by us, because we warned that the situation in Iraq was more complicated than the simplistic position put forward by imperialism, by Blair and Bush, but also, unfortunately, by others on the left such as the SWP.

Iraq is divided, as you said, into different ethnic and religious groups: Shias, Sunnis, Kurds, Turcomen – most of the Christians have fled because of persecution. Society has imploded absolutely into a 'near civil war'. We warned of this even before the Iraq war began. We said that Bush would be going into a Vietnam type of situation.[1] In the Sunni areas there is an Arab nationalist resistance to American imperialism, largely

1 - I wrote a book at the outset of the war drawing some parallels. Even Bush has now conceded that the Vietnam parallel with Iraq is valid. He also admitted that the military situation there is comparable to the 'Tet Offensive' in 1968 in the south of Vietnam. That was ultimately a military 'victory' for the US but a major political defeat; the American people turned decisively against the war. This paved the way for the first outright military defeat of US imperialism, after the 'draw' in Korea. This element of the Vietnam War – the Tet Offensive – is valid when related to the current situation in Iraq; the

in the middle belt of Iraq and some other isolated areas. It is composed, from what we can see from the outside, of elements of the Ba'athist party, ex-army officers, ordinary people, workers and peasants in opposition to the occupation, which is now overwhelmingly rejected, especially by the five million Sunnis. Then there are the jihadists, who are a minority as far as we can see, and who are tolerated by parts of the resistance, but are not supported or liked necessarily because of their methods: beheadings, indiscriminate suicide bombing, sectarian murders, etc.

The Sunni resistance by itself cannot successfully evict imperialism because it is a minority in Iraq. It can cause big difficulties by tying down foreign troops in a long-term and bloody occupation. The Shias were in opposition to Saddam because he persecuted them and used state terror to keep Iraq together. This came after the crushing of the left and the workers' movement. He kept the lid on the religious and national divisions in Iraq. But now that lid has been lifted, a Pandora's Box has been opened which has resulted in a catastrophe. The relationship between the different groups is confused but a tit-for-tat sectarian war is under way.

What are the likely perspectives for Iraq? Sections of the American ruling class are now saying this is an unwinnable war. There is no possibility of a military victory in Iraq. But what is the alternative? It is one thing to go into a quagmire, another to get out of it. This task is almost impossible. What we have in Iraq are a number of 'least worst' alternatives as far as American imperialism is concerned. There is no easy alternative. One perspective urged on the US is to hand over power to the Shia bourgeois parties. We do not agree with the SWP that al-Sadr's party represents a radical wing of Shi'ite politics. At one stage, he urged a kind of collaboration between the Sunni and the Shia resistance but that broke down and now religious conflict has become rooted.

The US generals' perspective before the invasion was to hand over power, to Chalabi or some other figure, hope for the best, and then withdraw to their 110 bases in Iraq. They went into Iraq for the oil reserves and they will not give up easily. If the US withdraws from Iraq without an independent working-class force in its place, the consequences for the rest of the Middle East are serious. There is a 'Shia arc' with big Shia populations in Iran, Iraq, Syria, Lebanon, parts of Saudi Arabia – where the Shias live in the areas where the oilfields are located – and the Gulf states. In some states, the Shias are a majority. If Iraq fractures on religious lines it will have enormous repercussions throughout the Middle East. The Iraqi people should decide their own fate.[2]

American people reject the war and Bush.
2 - In desperation, even the Republican Party 'establishment' is urging Bush to come to a deal with Iran and Syria, previously pariahs, Iran being part of the 'axis of evil'. Iran has been significantly strengthened as a regional power by the Iraq War, increasing its influence with their Shia co-religionists. The US hopes that Iran will lean on the Shias to prevent the break-up of Iraq but it is not certain they will succeed.

We support the legitimate, nationalist resistance of the Iraqi people against imperialism. We do not give uncritical support to any organisation in Iraq. The working class wants to know what their programme and policies are, whether they are prepared to reach out to the other religious and ethnic groups on a class basis. We suggest to Iraqi workers the idea of mixed militias, of Shias and Sunnis. Now the situation seems to be very polarised. Whether mixed militias are a possibility, we have to see but we have to suggest a way out on the lines of class unity. We are in favour of the withdrawal of all foreign troops from Iraq. But in the changed situation this will not automatically solve the situation. This is a complicated situation. We have to find a thread, a class and a socialist thread, which could reach out to the best workers.

At the moment, the class struggle is skewed by this sectarian nightmare. There have been some strikes amongst the oil workers. There have been strikes of workers in the north. We have to support this tender plant, especially those workers who resist privatisation and so on. At the same time, we have to put forward a political alternative, a general political alternative, which should include the demands for the withdrawal of all foreign troops; for a socialist, democratic confederation of Iraq with the right of self-determination for the Kurdish areas, the Sunni areas and the Shia areas if necessary; opposition to the privatisation programme; support for workers on strike. But it is not the most favourable position at the moment for the class struggle and socialism.

Vietnam and Iraq

I have read your book on Vietnam and the subtitle is 'the lessons for today'. When the war began, many people started to think that the situation in Iraq was similar to Vietnam. I always thought there were big differences. In Vietnam there was a typical national liberation war, with the support of a big power (USSR) whereas in Iraq the global economic situation now is far worse than at the time of Vietnam. What are the lessons for today?

I wrote the book on Vietnam on the eve of the Iraq War. There are general lessons but I think, paradoxically, the lessons of Vietnam apply more to Lebanon at this stage than they do to Iraq. In Lebanon we saw that, in an 'asymmetrical war', a big military power with huge advantages of personnel and arms could not defeat an indigenous national resistance movement, which is what Hezbollah became. Such a force has not existed up to now in Iraq – but in Lebanon it did, at least temporarily. Hezbollah did unite the different religious groups behind its resistance to the Israeli ruling class and the IDF. There is no such organisation in Iraq which is capable of acting in this fashion.

At the beginning of the Iraq War, while we saw the ethnic and religious divisions, nobody could predict exactly what would happen. We did say that an element of the Vietnam War could develop. Even if US imperialism or any other government decided to withdraw from the central provinces of Iraq – for instance, an American general has recently suggested that US troops should be withdrawn and based in the Kurdish areas – it would still leave the problem of five million Sunnis who would resist either a Shia-dominated government or American imperialism. The earlier example we gave of Northern Ireland has shown that, even though they enjoyed support only from a minority, the IRA could not be defeated militarily by British imperialism. There was a 30-year war. The same lessons apply as far as the Sunnis are concerned today. So that is one element of the lessons of Vietnam.

The lessons of the Vietnam War have been vindicated in Iraq in the sense that the mood of the American people after Vietnam was 'never again shall we be involved in a foreign war, especially against a nationalist resistance or guerrilla force'. The majority of the American population now say that the war was wrong and that the US should get out of the Middle East. We even have sections of the American ruling class, such as the former ambassador to Croatia, Peter Galbraith, saying quite simply that the US should evacuate its forces from Iraq. Also, in relation to Afghanistan, there is now a big section of the British bourgeoisie who say 'get out of Afghanistan'. When the British Empire existed it was not possible to defeat the Afghans, nor could the Russians defeat the Afghans with 150,000 troops. What chance has the NATO force of 25,000 troops, even given the medieval barbarism of the Taliban? In that sense, the lessons of Vietnam apply to Afghanistan and Iraq. On the other hand, they do not fully apply because there is not in Iraq one unified national resistance movement with majority support in the population.

Central Asia

Iraq is also in the centre of the Middle East and Central Asia, between big powers and regional powers struggling for control. There is the question of Afghanistan, which is becoming worse and worse. It is a poor country. There is the question of Pakistan. On the other side is Kazakhstan, rich in natural resources, Uzbekistan, where there was a rebellion last year. From Europe we look at the Iraqi situation as more connected to the Middle East but we want to look at its connections with Central Asia.

The relationship between the Middle East situation and the Central Asian situation, from the point of view of world capitalism and imperialism, is very simple. It is oil. The whole reason for the invasion of Iraq, despite all the attempts to cover it up, was that Iraq had the second largest oil reserves in the world. If they captured the oil of Iraq, Cheney, Wolfowitz and others said we will reduce the world price of oil to $6 a barrel. Energy plays a key role in capitalism. The oil price increase of 1974-75 was a trigger for the world economic crisis of that period, one of the factors at least. The rise in the price of oil to $70 or $80 a barrel has not yet triggered a crisis. But if Iran is bombed, it would block the Straits of Hormuz and that could raise the price of oil to $100 or even $150 a barrel and it would have a colossal effect on world capitalism. So oil is a connecting factor.

There is a geopolitical issue here too, in the sense that after 9/11 American imperialism has tried to extend its operations by establishing a firm base in Iraq. They have also extended their influence into the former spheres of influence of Russian Stalinism in Central Asia. The Caspian Sea is obviously an important area for its energy potential alone. Pakistan is crucial for the 'war on terror'. President Musharraf has revealed that Richard Armitage, who was an alleged 'liberal' in the Bush regime, a supporter of Colin Powell, told Musharraf after 9/11 that if he did not agree to the waging of a war against the Taliban in Afghanistan and allow Pakistan to be used as a base for this, the US would bomb Pakistan back into the Stone Age! Musharraf is saying this now because Bush is unpopular and he is looking towards the future. Pakistan is an important geopolitical factor as well, not just for the US and Western imperialism, but also China is trying to establish a sphere of influence. China is trying to create a counterweight to NATO in the form of the Shanghai Co-Operation Organisation, an 'Asian NATO'. It is trying to group together Asian capitalist nations as a counterweight to the US and even linking up with Russia as well.

There is another factor which is perhaps not posed in your question but which is important and that is the ramifications of the struggles in Iraq and the Middle East in general, and in Central Asia on the question of Islam and what is called 'Islamic fundamentalism'. We call this phenomenon 'right-wing political Islam'. In Hezbollah, there is an element of 'radical' Islam just beginning to appear but it should not be exaggerated. It is nowhere near the same as the radical Islamic ideas at the time of the Khomeini movement in the Iranian revolution, with its demand for a 'republic of the poor'. Ahmadi-Nejad is a populist and echoes a little the original aims of the Iranian Revolution at the present time. His radical populism involves support for the poor and criticism of the 1,000 families that control Iran. But at the same time, the regime has a repressive policy towards the working class, crushing the Tehran bus workers' strike, opposition to democratic rights in general. On the question of women, he is ambivalent. He is in favour of women being allowed to attend football matches but not to free them from the imposition of the chador and so on. So the question of right-wing political Islam and the Middle East does have a bearing on Central Asia.

Bob Labi: "One of the key issues at the moment is that there is not an independent workers' movement in Iraq. It is a very difficult situation. Where are the actual forces to start from? Obviously, US imperialism has got the main responsibility for what has happened in Iraq, with the invasion and war. But there was also the failure of the workers' movement as a result of the policies of the Stalinists. This led to the defeat of the Iraqi workers' movement. The whole opportunism of the CP in relation to the Ba'athist movement led to, first, the beheading of the workers' movement and then its destruction. That, I think is an important question. While each country is unique, in other countries similar situations have faced the workers' movement. If the workers' movement is not able to develop an independent role then it will lead not just to the defeat of the workers' movement but also the unravelling, the break-up of countries and the development of sectarian conflicts.

"Also, in a different way, this is one of the factors behind the development of right-wing political Islam. In many of these counties, it has been the failure of the workers' movement and, in some of the Arab countries, the failure of the bourgeois nationalist movements, which are important background features. It is not just historical but also could be posed in the future, in different ways, in other countries – the question of what the workers' movement actually does. From the point of view of the CWI, for example in India or in Nigeria, there are multinational or multi-ethnic states which could fracture. But the future for those particular states depends on what happens in the workers' movement and in future struggles. If the workers' movement fails in these countries, you could have the break up – every case is different – on national or religious lines. In Nigeria, there are thousands of people who have been killed in Muslim-Christian clashes. It has not happened in the big cities yet but it is a warning."

Leon Trotsky - Author of the theory of the permanent revolution

The Permanent Revolution Today

You speak about the new politics of imperialism, the national and ethnic problems, the question of democratic rights, the problems of the struggle for socialism in different countries, including semi-colonial countries. The last development of the theory of the permanent revolution was at the end of the 1920s in the polemics with the Comintern. But the Comintern was a mass force in the international arena, the working class was strong and at the beginning of the decade there had been the Baku conference, where the Third International not only put forward an analysis of the situation but also a strategy for colonial and semi-colonial political alternatives. Today, the situation is that the socialists and revolutionary Marxists are weak in the working class. How can the politics of the permanent revolution work? How can the political questions be answered and socialism as an alternative to terrorism be applied? In general it is a question of politics. How is the struggle against terrorism transformed? At the beginning of the 20th century there was a strong International with big sections. In the 1920s and 1930s, there was a degenerated International. Today, there is a very different situation. How does the permanent revolution work today?

The theory of the permanent revolution is over 100 years old. There has been a discussion in a recently published book between different academic Marxists about this theory, in support of Trotsky's ideas but, in my opinion, applying it in a very general abstract way to circumstances which do not pertain to what he was driving at. The theory of the permanent revolution is really about the revolution in an underdeveloped country with pre-capitalist tasks not yet completed. The bourgeois-democratic revolution in the neo-colonial world is not able to be completely carried through without the proletariat leading the poor and peasant masses. Once having come to power, the proletariat then goes over to the socialist tasks of the revolution, both nationally and internationally. That theory, in our opinion, applies today to the underdeveloped world. It could be said that, even in some of the semi-developed countries, there is an element of the bourgeois-democratic revolution not yet carried through; on the national question, for instance, which we discussed before. This task – the solution of the national question – can only be understood and carried through by an application of the theory of the permanent revolution.

Because of the absence of a strong, powerful, revolutionary working-class pole of attraction, in the post-1945 period, the theory of the permanent revolution was vindicated, for example, in the cases of China and Cuba but in a caricatured form, not in the classical schema laid down by Trotsky. It is also very applicable in the neo-colonial world today. The theory of stages, originally put forward by the Mensheviks, then by the Stalinists, and now by a variety of organisations in the neo-colonial world, comes into conflict with the idea and the programme of the permanent revolution.

It still retains its validity in countries like Sri Lanka, where the bourgeois-democratic revolution has not been fully carried out, on the national question, for instance. Nigeria is a bit different because, on the land question, there exists not just pre-capitalist but tribal elements, which are pre-feudal, as well as feudal elements in agriculture. There is the vital and explosive national question in Nigeria. It is only the working class that is capable of solving this, and that is a programmatic question. It is a huge issue in Nigeria and the religious and ethnic questions are also very complicated. All of those issues can only be solved not by basing oneself upon this or that ethnic group but by the working class in general playing a role in mobilising the peasant and rural masses. That is the classical idea of the permanent revolution in the underdeveloped world.

In Sri Lanka, there is the very powerful historical tradition of the Lanka Sama Samaja Party (LSSP). Alongside Bolivia and Vietnam before 1945, this is a successful example of a Trotskyist party able to have an implantation in the working class and, in turn, affecting the rural population. The LSSP was the first party founded in Sri Lanka, not just the first workers' party! The United National Party (UNP) and the Sri Lanka Freedom Party came later. The LSSP found a powerful echo within the working class. It did not start in the rural areas but amongst the working class and found a response in the rural areas; it always had a base amongst the farmers or peasants. In 1953, it organised a movement in the cities, a general strike supplemented by a movement in the rural areas through the *hartal*, an all-island form of struggle taken from India. This was a classic example of the permanent revolution in action. Marx wrote of a working-class, proletarian movement in the cities supplemented by the 'second edition' of the Peasants' War (from Germany in the 16th century). The *hartal* was an all-island strike of workers and peasants, although for a limited duration of one day. This magnificent movement prepared the way for the electoral defeat of the UNP in 1956.

The revolutions in China, Cuba and Vietnam were vindications of the theory of permanent revolution, not in its classical form but in a distorted fashion. The essence of Trotsky's theory of the permanent revolution was not just that the bourgeoisie could not solve the tasks of the bourgeois-democratic revolution. The working class could solve those tasks, but only a conscious revolutionary party like the Bolsheviks would be able to lead the nation, the majority of the workers and peasants that is, in the bourgeois-democratic tasks and go over to the international tasks, posing the question of socialism on a world scale. Lenin's original slogan was the 'democratic dictatorship of the proletariat and peasantry'. He was unsure who would dominate in the alliance, the peasantry or the working class. However, he came out decisively in his *April Theses* of April 1917 in agreement with Trotsky's position. But even his previous theory explained, in effect, that the 'democratic dictatorship' would provoke the international revolution which would then, in turn, come to the assistance of the Russian Revolution.

In China, the classical working-class revolution of 1925-27 failed because of the role of Stalin and his Chinese supporters. Mao Zedong's guerrillas in the countryside were an echo of that defeat. The 'Communist Party' under Mao, it is generally accepted now, was not a conscious Bolshevik or clear Marxist force. It was really a peasant army in the tradition of China, where peasant armies had struggled, overcame the landlords, entered the cities and created a new dynasty. Then the cycle would begin again without the underlying problems being resolved. In China between 1927 and 1944, and then to 1949, Chinese landlordism and capitalism had shown its complete bankruptcy under Chiang Kai-shek. It capitulated to Japanese imperialism, China was divided into the fiefdoms of the different warlords and there was no way forward. Then this peasant army of ex-communists took power – they used the terminology of Marxism but were not in the tradition of Lenin, Trotsky and the Bolsheviks, a conscious working-class force.

There is a big debate amongst sinologists, even those from a Trotskyist background, some of whom say the Trotskyists in China made a mistake. They should have gone into the countryside and gone with Mao. I do not accept or support that. Historically, the road to the peasantry for Marxists in the first instance is through support amongst the working class. Because the working class is linked to the peasantry, in that way it finds a road to the rural masses. That was the position of Lenin and Trotsky in the Russian Revolution. Trotsky makes the point on Mao's 'Red Army' that it was a peasant army. We saw the mentality of a peasant army in the Russian Revolution and the civil war. Makhno and the anarchists' armies, who stood between the Reds and the Whites, were hostile to the Whites because they represented the landlords. But they also clashed with the Reds because they represented the 'city' and the working class, and were perceived as a threat to the peasants, particularly the rich peasants.

Trotsky posed the question in relation to China: would it not be most likely that if Mao won and entered the cities then his Red Army could come into collision with the working class, who might begin to rise and form its own organisations, soviets and so on, as they did between 1925 and 1927? Trotsky was very perceptive because, when Mao was about to enter the cities, the Red Army produced leaflets saying nobody must strike – anybody who took an independent position would be met with repression. This was a typical Bonapartist leadership based on a peasant army with an expressed fear of the independent movement of the working class. There was no real communist, Trotskyist, Marxist appeal to the working class to support the peasants.

Trotsky envisaged that the Red Army could enter the cities, come into collision with the working class and, in that situation, there would be a new dynasty formed and the cycle would begin all over again. But it did not happen in that way. Because of the bankruptcy of landlordism and capitalism there was a huge vacuum. Mao came into the cities and balanced between the different classes. He did not come out for a 'socialist' state or a workers' state or anything like that initially. In fact, he talked about a 'national democracy' involving sections of the national bourgeoisie. Chiang Kai-shek, his army, the capitalists and the landlords fled. There was no other armed force and Mao balanced between the classes. Mao started where Stalin had finished by creating from the outset a Stalinist state. He carried through, over a period, the liquidation of landlordism, began to take over industry and created a workers' state, which was 'deformed' from the beginning. There were no soviets and other elements of workers' democracy. Nevertheless, this was a vindication of the permanent revolution but in a caricaturised form. In a similar fashion, Stalinism did the same thing, in a way, in Eastern Europe although with some important differences. A Stalinist state was created from the beginning. This was a planned economy but with a one-party regime. Trotskyists in China were imprisoned, some of them remaining in prison for 20 or 30 years, but the Chinese Revolution was a vindication of the theory of the permanent revolution in the sense that landlordism and capitalism in the neo-colonial world cannot solve the problems of the bourgeois-democratic revolution, even in the era of imperialism.

In some countries, like Japan, the bourgeois-democratic revolution was completed from the top under imperialist occupation. In Japan, US General MacArthur carried through land reform which liquidated the remaining elements of feudalism. This was in order to develop Japan as a bastion against Chinese Stalinism. The same in Taiwan. Chiang Kai-shek could not carry through land reform in China, dependent as he was on the landlords, but in Taiwan he expropriated the domestic Taiwanese landlords and capitalists, and in the process laid the basis for a developed capitalist structure.

The theory of the permanent revolution was again vindicated in the case of Vietnam. This was a clear national liberation struggle based on the peasantry in the main but, again, why did it result in a social revolution? Because there was no way forward on the basis of capitalism in Vietnam. When the NLF – the Vietcong – came to power, North and South were reunified. They carried through land reform, established a workers' state. However, afterwards, the new regime began to introduce elements of capitalism into Vietnam. Nevertheless, in the first instance, the theory of permanent revolution was vindicated but in a distorted way.

Cuba was a similar case but slightly different because of the origins of the Cuban Revolution. I will not go into all the details here as we have done so in our book. When Fidel Castro and Guevara came to power, contrary to what he says today, Castro was not a Marxist. His model was the United States. He said subsequently that it was a manoeuvre! This was to fool US imperialism. Che Guevara was from a Communist Party tradition and so was Raúl Castro but not Fidel Castro. The revolution was based on the guerrilla struggle of a small group initially. The guerrillas were not a working-class movement, they were based upon the rural masses. Only after the Cuban Revolution had succeeded in the sense that Batista was already fleeing did the masses of Havana organise a general strike. It was a most peculiar 'deformed workers' state' in the sense that it was, at the beginning, outside the Stalinist tradition, which Mao was not. Cuba was an entirely new development. There were elements of workers' control, and there was the huge popularity of Castro and Guevara themselves. They moved towards the expropriation of Cuban capitalism and American imperialism, step by step.

South Africa

In the 1970s and 1980s, the revolutionary left in general said that there was only one road for South Africa. They were the best conditions for the vindication of the permanent revolution. After, the process did not confirm the permanent revolution. How do you explain this very typical situation for the vindication of the permanent revolution?

It was correct to say in the 1970s and the 1980s that in South Africa the democratic tasks – one person, one vote, etc – were revolutionary demands in the context of apartheid. It could only be achieved by the application of the theory of the permanent revolution, a socialist revolution. The black working class, if mobilised on a revolutionary programme through an uprising, would smash the apartheid regime, grant democratic rights and go over to the tasks of the socialist revolution, not just in South Africa but in the African continent as a whole. That was a correct appraisal of this theory but it is again a question of the change of circumstances in world political factors. In the past, the South African regime had refused to budge under the pressure of imperialism. Harold Macmillan, the former British prime minister, made his famous 'winds of change' speech in Cape Town in 1959. This was a warning to the white minority regimes that they would have to give way and retreat in the face of mass African resistance to them.

But they refused to heed Macmillan's advice and battened down the hatches. They introduced more discriminatory and dictatorial measures against the black African masses, the 'coloureds' and their supporters in the white population. This assumed that the ANC would be compelled, under pressure, to lead the revolution or it would split in the process and a revolutionary wing would emerge. That was the general perspective that we put forward. In fact, we had a general discussion in our ranks at the time when some in our South African organisation argued there could be democratic reform from the top by somebody like Buthelezi, who would be handed power by the white capitalist elite and that would open the gates to a form of truncated, strangulated capitalism with a black face leading it. In reality, power would still be vested in the hands of the whites. We discounted that possibility in the 1970s and 1980s.

But there were big underlying changes in the 1980s and those changes led to the collapse of Stalinism and the abandonment of revolutionary or even quasi-revolutionary phraseology by Stalinism. For example, Russian Stalinism in the 1960s supported Cuba, without which the Cuban regime could not have existed for more than a few months. It depended on oil from Russia. In the later case of Nicaragua, however, they consciously put pressure on the Sandinistas not to break with capitalism and so did Castro. The same in Ghana with Rawlings. The acceptance of the results of a revolution, as with Cuba, by the Stalinist states was an expensive luxury they were no longer prepared to support.

There was also evidence in the 1980s, on the part of a section of the bureaucracy, of a move back towards capitalism. With the collapse of the Soviet Union, those trends and tendencies were magnified. Mandela and the bourgeois wing of the ANC pushed towards the right. The Congress of South African Trade Unions (COSATU) had arisen as a revolutionary trade union – *amandla!* (power) – and we helped in its formation. It was a revolutionary threat. We could give many examples of the African workers talking about the revolution, of needing to 'kill' trade union leaders who were not prepared to support the revolution. That was the natural reaction of the African workers in the underground, especially the mineworkers. It was a struggle to the end. It was socialism and the revolution; it was particularly the case as far as young people were concerned.

But the situation changed with the collapse of Stalinism and the recognition by the white regime of de Klerk that they could open up from the top and maybe have a power-sharing arrangement with the ANC. The fundamental economic interests of capitalism would not be threatened because of the shift towards the right of the ANC leadership under the pressure of the collapse of Stalinism and also the release of Mandela. Mandela had long discussions before he was released in which the ground was obviously prepared for him to play this role; in effect, to betray the revolution.

Africa

Bob Labi: "I think there is another side to this. The permanent revolution involves an analysis of why these countries, especially in Africa and parts of Asia and Latin America, are not developed. Why in parts of Africa is society actually going backwards? Why have the movements which existed and developed, whether it is the workers' movement in some countries or even some of the bourgeois national-ist movements, failed to carry out the tasks? This can be explained in terms of the objective conditions which make the permanent revolution necessary and also the failure of the different organisations to have the sort of programme to carry through the revolution. Instead, they propose the 'stages theory' in different forms.

"So it is not just a question of the programme that is necessary, it is also the analysis which explains why countries do not develop. We can give the example of Nigeria. Why is Nigeria, a country of 120-130 million people, with a huge amount of natural resources and wealth, not developing and instead is going backwards? It can be explained by the grip of imperialism and also weakness of local capitalism. How do you break that? In a country like Nigeria there is a potentially powerful working class but it has not been able to achieve its aims.

"As we have been saying all along, conditions are always changing. In the 1990s with the development of the Asian Tigers, there was a discussion in different countries of the neo-colonial world: could they also become Tigers? To a certain extent the crisis at the end of the 1990s put a stop to that discussion. But now, with the development of China and, to some extent, India, the question is posed in some countries: could we follow the Chinese road? It is a new form of the discussion on the Asian Tigers. Is it possible in Africa for a country to develop like China? That is a discussion which is now taking place in India. Can India develop in the same way as China has developed? These are things we have to consider and we are not closing our eyes to the developments taking place but looking at how dependent they are on the developments in the world economy and also the question of the relative strengths of the different imperialist powers.

"In Africa, which is a special case, the question of China is also something which is not always an attraction but can be the opposite amongst sections of the masses. In Nigeria, there is a mounting explosion of anger towards China, which is seen as coming in and taking the resources. Also, local African companies are closed down as a result of competition from China. There is also a racial element which I discovered when in Nigeria last year. Workers think that Chinese employers are worse than Western bosses because they are more brutal. I was surprised by the hostility, not just of CWI members but of many other workers, to Chinese employers. They considered that they are far worse than the Europeans because at least the Europeans would recognise token trade unions. The Chinese do not care; they just get the police sent in immediately if workers struggle."

The permanent revolution can be vindicated in a positive way by the victory of the working class in Russia, but so also in a negative sense by the failure of revolutions: in China 1925-27, and in other circumstances in the neo-colonial world. But even in South Africa, what we had as a result of the permanent revolution not being applied consciously by the working class through its organisations was an abortion of a regime. We have a society in which some features of apartheid still exist in the discrimination, the housing, the divisions even between sections of the African masses and the 'coloured' masses. South Africa experienced a derailed revolution.

We knew South African comrades in the 1980s who discussed with us in our headquarters in London – revolutionaries participating in the struggles of the mineworkers' union. One of these, Irene Charnley, is now one of the richest black women in South Africa because of the opportunities which opened up for a black African elite. People like Cyril Ramaphosa, a former leader of the mineworkers' union and now a rich businessman, have copies of Trotsky's books which were given to them by members of our party when they had been radicalised by the revolution. But in the new situation that opened up with the release of Mandela, they shifted towards the right. Mandela was always more on the right of the ANC than on the left. These people, as a result of 'black empowerment' for an elite not the masses, then gave a cover to the same predominantly capitalist set-up in South Africa. However, the revolutionary drive and potential is there amongst the working class, which will break out again.

The Working Class Today

In the 1990s, there was a big ideological attack from the bourgeoisie with the claim that the working class no longer existed! This ideological attack was a sign of a real process. Before the process of globalisation began, there was the process of deindustrialisation in many countries. In Milan there used to be ten factories of 20,000 workers but there is not one now. The concentration of workers allowed organisation into the trade unions. The problems and difficulties that we have had as revolutionaries but also amongst the reformist left were the result of the deindustrialisation and changes in capitalism in Western European countries. You now have workers in offices of 20 people; there is a different working class. Most of the far left before, such as Lutte Ouvrière in France, was workerist. The industrial workers were the central contingent of the working class and the revolution. What do you think about the transformation and the role of the industrial working class?

It is indisputable that the process of deindustrialisation is common throughout Europe, Japan and the US, and even in the neo-colonial world in countries like Brazil, in Latin America and Africa. Factories are closed and the work outsourced to China, where the labour is cheaper. We have to view this question from an international standpoint. The world working class and the industrial working class on the world scale is still key, although the industrial workers are not necessarily in the 'industrialised' countries. That is why China, India and countries where there has been a certain development are so important. The outsourcing of factories to Eastern Europe and Russia will assume importance in the next period, although relocation there is not on the scale of China. Of course, not all value and surplus value is created by the 'industrial' workers nor do all these workers reside in China and other parts of Asia. There are new layers of the working class who are also productive and the working class in general is still dominant in Europe, the US and Japan.

But deindustrialisation is a conscious or semi-conscious policy on the part of the bourgeoisie. That was particularly the case in Britain, in which the process of deindustrialisation and the replacement of industrial capitalism by rentier capitalism, as Lenin put it, has gone much further than anywhere else, at least in Europe. The decline of manufacturing and industrial jobs in Britain is much greater than, for instance, in Germany or France, and perhaps even more than in Italy. Industrial workers are a higher percentage of the workforce in Italy than in Britain, where there are only 3.8 million manufacturing workers. We have to include amongst industrial workers those in transport and in extractive industries. Nevertheless, the industrial working class has shrunk.

Thatcher pursued a conscious policy of deindustrialisation that has some similarities to that of the French bourgeoisie following the Paris Commune. After the fright of the Paris Commune, Lenin pointed out, the French bourgeoisie deliberately held back the development of industry in France and developed a rentier capitalism based upon their colonies. It exported capital, extracted the surplus from their colonies but held back the development of industry and, therefore, the proletariat in France because of the social threat that it posed. This lasted for 100 years. Only under de Gaulle in the ten years he was in power did a big industrialisation take place and the agricultural labour reserves of France were used up.

There is an element of this now in the consciousness of the bourgeoisie of Western Europe to try and weaken the proletariat by relocating industry, or threatening to do so. In some countries now, the industrial working class is a minority of the working class, which is the case in Britain. The amount of cars produced in Britain is roughly the same as in the 1970s but this is done with a much smaller workforce and mostly foreign-owned companies. There is no British-owned mass car manufacturer now. On the other hand, the process of neo-liberalism has meant that sections of the workforce who previously did not consider themselves as part of the working class have been proletarianised. Civil servants in Britain, teachers, social workers and other workers of that character have changed their outlook from previous periods. In Britain, one of the most left-wing trade unions is the Public and Commercial Services Union (PCS) in which the Socialist Party has significant influence on the National Executive Committee and at all levels of the union. Teachers, at the present time, work in schools which are becoming factory-like. Schools used to be collaborative. Teachers would have a vocational attitude. But no more! The head teacher of a school is like the manager of a factory, often with the same kind of brutal attitude towards the workforce. In a broad sense, in the workplace there has been a 'proletarianisation' and also from a social point of view.

Therefore, what we are dealing with is a new working class. Industrial workers and transport workers are still a very important component of the working class. But they are complemented by the new sections – white-collar workers and others. Even though the industrial working class can be small in number, its specific weight within industry can be as great if not greater than in the past. One of the biggest labour forces in London is that of the workers at Heathrow airport, made up of many grades but with quite harsh conditions. This is a very important part of the London working class now. Many are migrant workers or former immigrant labour.

The working class is not disappearing but taking on a different form. Increasingly, it is not the classical working class of Marx and Engels, in Europe, Japan and the US. But the working class is a majority of society. In the past, British society was heavily proletarianised. Italy became proletarianised in the post-1945 period. But in the space of two generations, a huge agricultural reserve of labour shifted into industry. The masses were dragged up from the South and forced into great, inhuman factories, into dreary housing blocks, radicalised and revolutionised. Now, workers are thrown out of the factories into other, tertiary occupations. In Britain, car workers ejected from the factories get jobs in the service sector but at half the rates of pay they had before.

There are many factors here which are acting to radicalise, or potentially radicalise, the working class. The industrial working class is smaller but nevertheless can be crucial. We include railway workers amongst the industrial working class. The Rail, Maritime and Transport Union (RMT) can bring the whole of London to a halt by a strike on the tubes and trains, which means they occupy a big specific weight. But civil servants can also, by a strike, bring the whole of the government machinery to a halt. There is also the involvement of women who are a majority of the labour force in Britain now, which is a huge, potentially revolutionising factor. There are also new general theoretical questions which are thrown up such as the ideas of Marx on productive and non-productive labour. I think that is an important theoretical issue which has a certain bearing on the world situation today.

Where is the majority of the surplus value now created by world capitalism? Does it still come from industry in Europe, Japan and the US, or has it been transferred to China? What does that mean for the future? At the moment the 'triad' of Europe, Japan and the US collectively, because of their technological superiority, especially the US, are able to relocate and extract the surplus from China and Eastern Europe. This is then partly used by the triad to try and stabilise their home bases. British capitalism, for instance, has a deficit on its balance of trade which is the second worst since the 18th century but, because of its investments abroad, the tribute which it extracts from this plugs the gap.

New layers

The working class and proletariat has changed in consciousness, I mean not just political consciousness. Today, there is militarisation. There are many

unemployed people and some who retire early because of the benefits. Young people work in call centres with low wages. Capitalism has more profits in China but here they demand lower and lower wages. The capitalists introduce new technology but the ability of the working class to buy this falls. How has the ideology of capitalism over the working class changed? The ideology of the ruling class is not just from a political point of view but, through lifestyle. It more and more penetrates different parts of life and not only in production or the relationship to work.

This is an attempt at the 'individualisation' of society: each worker becomes an individual and the collective is lost. There is no doubt that there is a conscious policy to 'atomise', ideologically at least, the working class. Up to a point, and for a period, that can succeed because there is a problem of huge alienation now. Alienation, as Marx pointed out, is a product of capitalist society. There are few big workforces. There is the growth of home working. Where do workers come together in common struggle? Psychological and mental problems flow from that, because human beings are social animals. We have to address those difficult issues. But I think there are limits to it as well.

This situation can even produce a certain lumpenisation and disintegration of society. It was expressed by Thatcher, who said, "There is no such thing as society." That is a conscious ideological approach: to scatter the working class politically and to dissipate its collective force. Perhaps when the system is going ahead, even inching ahead, it can succeed. When it jams and breaks down, when there are wars and ruptures, 'individuals' and groups begin to ask questions and that is where the political possibilities come in. By this attempt at individualisation, the bourgeoisie is loosening the bonds which bind the masses to the system; the ship's moorings have gone, the anchor has been lifted and people are casting around for alternatives, and that produces a crisis of politics as well. 'There is no alternative, where is the alternative? They are all the same!' This is the mood of significant sections of workers. It can produce, in the first instance, a kind of nihilism, anarchist ideas and so on amongst young people, but it is a phase. It is the first wave before the working class, or at least sections of it, begin to draw conclusions and then are forced to move, which will have an effect on other sections of workers.

France

New layers of the working class have arrived in the last period. There is no more work in big factories. There are many difficulties in organising and fighting. There were two different interesting situations in France: the riots

in November and the battle against the CPE (*Contrat Première Embauche* – first employment contract) in the spring. What do you think about these struggles and is it possible to see similar struggles in other countries? What was your view of the riots because there are very different positions inside the revolutionary left. For example, Lutte Ouvrière (LO) said the youth were not proletarians, they burn the cars of the proletariat; LO was outside and had no relationship with this rebellion. The Ligue Communiste Révolutionnaire (LCR) had quite a different position but was in many ways reformist. So I would like your judgement of this rebellion. Secondly, can the movement against the CPE be repeated in other countries?

The events in France are very important, not just for the French labour movement and the working class, but for Europe and the world. It is highly symptomatic of the general situation that is developing throughout the continent. In eight days at the end of March and beginning of April, there were two national demonstrations of three million people! That is extremely significant. The second point is that in the movement of the students and young people against the CPE, it was notable that the students, despite their lack of a revolutionary consciousness in general, instinctively turned towards the working class. The working class also understood the importance of this movement.

In these events, it was not 1968 *per se* but there was an element of 1968. In a way, it was more advanced than 1968 in the initial period. In 1968, there was the movement of the students, which came into collision with the Gaullist state. Despite the Communist Party, the working class linked up, defended the students from the police and then independently occupied the factories. This smashed a lot of the theories which were circulating in the far left at that time. In particular, the theory of the students as the 'detonator', put forward by ultra-left groups and even by some of the Trotskyists, such as the USFI, was erroneous. The student movements were symptomatic of the situation developing in French society but they were not an independent factor. You only have to compare France in 1968 to Germany. The extraparliamentary movement in Germany was on a higher plane and more developed than in France but it did not have the same echo amongst the working class in Germany as in France because the conditions were different.

The whole situation in France had matured under Gaullism and those events culminated in the greatest general strike in history with ten million workers occupying the factories. It did not happen like this in 2006 largely because of the leadership of the students and the workers, and also because of their undeveloped consciousness. There was a lack of a general socialist alternative unlike the broad socialist consciousness of

1968. This was not present in the movement of Spring 2006. But there were two mass demonstrations of three million people. The students linked up with the working class, and the working class understood that the attack on the students was an attack on them and their conditions. These were indications of the enormous potential.

Also important is the way that these events in France were understood internationally and were taken up. In Chile, in the movement of the school and university students, it was understood that the reason why the movement in France forced the government to step back, temporarily at least, was the involvement of the working class. So they turned to the Chilean working class and the unions. We have a section of the CWI in Chile which participated in these events. In Greece, where the CWI has an important presence amongst the school and university students, and has developed significantly in the course of the last few years, the New Democracy government had got away with so many attacks on the working class. But like the bourgeois generally everywhere in a situation like this, they overreached themselves. They launched a vicious attack on education, the students reacted and began to push aside the conservative student leadership. We posed the need to turn towards the working class, which they did, the question of the general strike was put on the agenda and a public-sector strike did take place.

So those two movements showed the colossal importance of the developments in France which is still, from the point of view of the class struggle, the most developed political situation in Europe at this stage. This is because of the objective situation but also because of the traditions and role of the French working class. The revolt of March and April forced the bourgeoisie to step back and there is a bubbling discontent that could break out again.

The upheavals in the *banlieues*, the suburbs, were an extremely important movement as well. There is endemic, mass unemployment of the young people, particularly in these areas. Those French youth in the *banlieues* are the sons and daughters of immigrants from North and sub-Saharan Africa in the main, though not exclusively. Given that 'ghettoes' exist, it is inevitable that flare-ups of this character will take place. The role of Marxists is not to hold up our hands in horror because this is not a perfect movement. This is a symptom of the incapacity of capitalism to absorb the most important productive force, which is the working class. It is compounded by the vicious racism against these youth and their parents, and the repression by the police and the bourgeois state in these areas.

It is not the first time nor will it be the last, when the working-class movement does not show a way forward, that inchoate, almost nihilistic, anarchistic moods will develop. Even in the Russian Revolution prior to October, when the Bolsheviks were becoming the majority in Petrograd, Trotsky made the point that there was a mood of impatience growing amongst a section of the working class. If the working class had not taken power – in the window of opportunity roughly between September and November 1917 – then the anarchists would have grown and the Bolsheviks would have fallen back. Ultra-leftism, anarchist and nihilistic moods are always payment for the opportunism of the leaders of the labour and trade union movement, and this movement was no different.

We have had experience of this in Britain. We had the uprisings, because that is what they were, of the populations of Brixton and then Liverpool 8, Toxteth, in 1981. We were involved in the sense that we tried to give it a positive direction. In the Brixton riots of 1981, Clare Doyle became a major spokesperson, known as 'red Clare' in the media. Our attitude was to say that the reason for that uprising was the neglect of these areas, the discrimination, the role of the police and so on. We demanded certain reforms in the area. We also pointed out to the youth that this was not the way to fight: 'Don't fight individually in single combat against the capitalist state. You should get organised and link up with us, with the working class and the labour movement in a conscious struggle against capitalism.'

The same approach should have been adopted by the far left in France. Lutte Ouvrière took a 'purist' and, therefore, erroneous position. It is entirely wrong to think that everything outside of a movement of the industrial working class in its 'pure' form is unimportant. What about white-collar workers? In the process of the decay of capitalism, *déclassé* layers can grow, even semi-lumpen layers like in the US in the 1960s in the conditions that existed amongst the black population. Nevertheless, we saw the rise of the Black Panthers, the anniversary of whom we are now marking. It was a marvellous testimony to socialism and Marxism that Huey Newton, Bobby Seale and others organised about one million people who considered themselves revolutionaries. These were not classical industrial workers in the main but they could have been an important lever for developing a base amongst the working class movement.

We do not stand aside from the youth in the French *banlieues*. We say to them that cars should not be burned, nor should white youth who are sympathetic to you be mugged and attacked. That is nihilism which will alienate other workers. But our first duty is to criticise the bourgeois state and police for their repressive methods and not to stand aside from the movement. Lutte Ouvrière was entirely wrong in their stance but even the LCR were passive in the first period and did not intervene in the areas to criticise the police, probably because the bourgeois press presented it as a dangerous movement threatening ordinary working-class people, their cars and property. We intervened to demand a withdrawal of the police from the areas and came out sharply against Sarkozy and the bourgeois state who were calling these youth 'scum'. Even black footballers like Lilian Thuram, the Juventus player at the time, reacted, saying: 'I come from these areas – what right has Sarkozy to intervene and condemn people like me who come from these areas as scum?'

If capitalist society goes into crisis and there is not a conscious organisation of the working class, including unemployed layers, there could be uprisings of this character taking place again. What should our attitude be? We have to try and base ourselves on the working class involved in production, it is true, because from here will come the main forces. But it would be absolutely fatal to ignore these other layers. If they are white, they can be open to exploitation by the fascists; and if they are the descendants of North African immigrants, they can be open to the ideas of right-wing political Islam. It is the duty of Marxists, Trotskyists and the labour movement to intervene and to try and reach them with our ideas.

Bob Labi: "There are two other things. If the workers' movement does not actually provide a lead to some of these youth, as we saw, unfortunately, in some of the student demonstrations attacks can take place on them by lumpenised youth. The police allow these attacks to take place – how much they were provoked and instigated is a different question – by mainly immigrant youth simply to rob some of the school students who were on the demonstrations. And that is a warning, a small warning, that if the workers' movement does not offer a way out, some of these youth could end in a *cul-de-sac*. It is a generalised situation because if you look at the present economic boom in most countries of Western Europe, let alone Eastern Europe, there are very high levels of youth unemployment, high levels of youth in temporary, precarious jobs; all of which could fuel this element of frustration.

"The other point which I think is important about France is that the movement which started this year actually came from below. If it had been left to the workers' leaders, nothing would have happened. Last year, in the summer of 2005, the French government passed a similar law, the CNE (*Contrat Nouvelle Embauche* – New Employment Contract), for all workplaces. Workers who started a job in any small workplace with less than 20 workers could be sacked at any time in the first year of employment. This year's new legislation was to extend the law from just small workplaces to youth under 25. What happened last year was that, when the first law was passed, the trade union leaders protested but did absolutely nothing and the law was put into effect. A layer of the youth drew the conclusion that they had to actually start from below if they were to stop the CPE. Many workers had seen what happened in 2005 and they were especially receptive to the idea of action from below, not just on this measure against the youth but also against the other measure, the CNE. So an important demand was raised in the movement, not just to stop the CPE aimed at the under-25s, but also to end the CNE passed in 2005.

"What was significant is that the trade union leaders fought against including the issue of the CNE in the demands. They deliberately acted to prevent it being included with the result that, while the French government retreated on the CPE, the CNE law is still in place. But the important thing is that youth and elements of working-class activists saw the need for spontaneous action because they could not rely just on the leaders of the trade unions."

Another point which is important is the consciousness of the young people and of the working class. The leaders of the youth and student movement, many of whom are influenced by the French Socialist Party, at least at an official, national level, made a point of saying that they were not revolutionary, they were not Marxists. They were not like the leaders of 1968 such as Krivine and Cohn-Bendit, who declared that they were revolutionaries. In the recent movement, the young people and the working class as well know what they do not want: neo-liberal capitalism, especially when it affects them in such a sharp fashion. But they are not clear as to the alternative.

The alternative model is not there as it was in the sense of the broad socialist consciousness which existed in the 1960s, 1970s and 1980s. In our opinion, that is linked to the collapse of Stalinism and the ideological offensive that the bourgeoisie has conducted for the last 15 years. It will take a combination of events and big events, and the conscious intervention of what hopefully will be a growing Marxist, Trotskyist force before that consciousness begins to change decisively as far as the mass is concerned. That does not mean to say there is not a layer of advanced, more developed younger people and workers who are open and receptive today to the ideas of Marxism and Trotskyism.

Relationship of class forces

The next question is about Europe in general. In our discussions in Italy, we have begun to discuss in the last year or two the general situation of the relationship of our forces in Europe and we have the impression that in the last 20 to 25 years there has been a retreat of the working class amongst the bigger sections of the working class in Europe. There have been other big movements, but in general the relationship of forces was not so bad, for instance, at the beginning of this century. There were defeats for the working class in England and in other countries. But there were many social-democratic and centre-left governments which opened the road to imperialist positions, but in general we always had big resistance movements against neo-liberalism's plans – for example, the movements in France and Italy. The irony is that there were big struggles against centre-right governments but not against centre-left governments. We think the relationship of forces between the classes has not changed deeply and the working class has not suffered a strong defeat as in the 1930s. Of course, the far right has made some gains but have never presented themselves as traditional fascists, so we have the possibility of thinking hard about how to change the relationship to new and fresh layers of the working class. What do you think of our position?

I think there are many aspects of that which we would agree with. But we have to try as far as possible to situate our conclusions in a general historical framework and the stage through which the labour movement passes at certain periods. For instance, it is quite clear that there was enormous radicalisation, let us put it no more than that – elements of a pre-revolutionary situation – in the 1970s in Italy and in France in 1968. In Britain, the miners defeated the Tories in 1972 and 1974; industrial action led to a general election in 1974 which brought down Heath's Tory government.

But we disagree with the analysis that has been made by some who try to neatly compartmentalise historical periods and misread, in the process, what took place. For instance, if you look at the analysis of the International Socialist Tendency (IST) they say there was a generally favourable situation between 1968 and 1976: France 1968; Italy; the overthrow of Franco, the collapse of the Caetano regime in Portugal and of the Greek colonels' regime. It was a favourable period for Marxists. But that does not mean to say that, following 1976, there was a period of quiescence or defeat of the movement. We saw in Britain, for instance, the defeat of Labour in 1979 and the coming to power of the Thatcher government. In the words of Karl Marx, this was the whip of the counter-revolution which stirred up a huge revolt of the British working class.

One of the most important events in British history, without a doubt, was the miners' strike of 1984-85. We participated fully in that and we made big gains. We recruited 500 miners to Militant in the course of that battle. We led the battle in Liverpool. The whole of the 1970s and 1980s were a period of enormous ferment. There was the beginning of the neo-liberal phase of capitalism. This did not develop as a conscious policy of the bourgeoisie but arose out of capitalist developments at the time. There was a boom following the crisis of 1979-81. We adjusted our political perspectives. But in general it was a very radical period. In this period, the

SWP/IST argued that it was not a favourable period and, consequently, they largely stood aside and waited on events. We fully participated in the miners' strike, which was defeated but has left its stamp on the consciousness of the British working class right up to today. The defeat, in the main, arose from the role of the Labour and trade union leaders. We had the expulsion of the Militant Editorial Board and the Liverpool Militants from the Labour Party. But notwithstanding this, we had the massive poll tax battle in which we defeated the government and Thatcher herself. She admitted that it was the defeat of the poll tax which brought her down. Eighteen million people refused to pay the poll tax. This was organised by Militant, through the All-Britain Anti-Poll Tax Federation.

I think that your analysis is basically correct about the current situation. But we also have to see what the basis is for this. It comes back to the question of 1989-90. For those who have a state capitalist position in relation to the regimes of the Soviet Union and Eastern Europe, their collapse was not a historic defeat for the working class but a 'sideways move'. We think that planned economies, bureaucratically managed, did exist. Only the outlines of a planned economy remained at the end but its liquidation was a historic defeat because these states represented an antici-pation of what could be possible on the basis of workers' democracy after pushing aside the bureaucracy. Their collapse gave the bourgeoisie the opportunity to conduct a huge ideological campaign which had a big effect.

The SWP/IST position was that it was a 'sideways move', that another form of capital-ism had merely taken over. This embroils them in all kinds of contradictions. Cliff came forward with the idea that this was a radical revolutionary period. It did give the opportunity for Marxists, following the discrediting of the communist parties, to make gains. But it was not the '1930s in slow motion' as he claimed! To describe the 1990s in this way is like the fool in a Russian proverb who sings a wedding song at a funeral and a funeral dirge at a wedding! The 1990s was a period of ideological reaction, which witnessed an orgy of pro-capitalist, pro-market, anti-working class and anti-socialist propaganda. It had a detrimental effect on the class struggle and the workers' movement, to put it mildly. It was not the most favourable period for Marxists. In fact, the SWP/IST is now in practice in the process of jettisoning that idea because they have come up against reality and have consequently moved rightwards. Temporarily, it gave their cadres a kind of fanatical energy to recruit very quickly a layer of young people who were soon lost. But they came up against a brick wall, as inevitably happens in politics if you have a wrong perspective and your cadres are not prepared.

We have to call things by their right names. We said that the working class worldwide had experienced a big defeat. When there is a defeat, recognise it. By all means do not draw unduly pessimistic conclusions for the future. If it had been a defeat like the triumph of Mussolini, Hitler and fascism in the interwar period, we would have said so, and we would have then concluded that we were in for a long period of difficulties. That was not the case. The organisations of the working class were not crushed but basically remained intact. The potential power of the working class, their ability to struggle, was retained. But their political outlook was confused. The bourgeoisie launched an ideological barrage. The *Wall Street Journal* had a headline at the beginning of the 1990s: "We won!" Capitalism, they maintained, had defeated 'socialism' and the idea of a planned economy. This coalesced with the beginning of a boom and the effects of neo-liberalism. This had an important effect.

Why is it in this period that the bourgeois workers' parties have largely disappeared from the map? Why has it had the effect of confusing the consciousness of the proletariat? Why were Marxist forces thrown back in numbers, influence and so on? We think we have maintained a very important position but this was a difficult historical situation. This was the result of the ideological campaign. But Marxists have to have a sense of proportion. The conclusion we came to was not that we had to pull up the drawbridge, retreat to the study, go 'underground' and wait for a new favourable situation in the future. We had a dual task of continuing to put forward the revolutionary programme but, at the same time, seeking to rehabilitate in a broad sense the ideas of socialism, Marxism and Trotskyism. One was directed at the advanced layer, the other for the broad mass.

With the political decay of the mass workers' parties, we very quickly said the Labour Party was finished as such a party, although that was not our position when we came out of the Labour Party. The same process of bourgeoisification would take place within other social-democratic parties in Europe. The Socialist Party in Italy under Craxi became completely bourgeoisified earlier than the rest - in fact it was in many ways a model for New Labour - before finally disappearing from the map, in the early 1990s. This process has now affected the DS and the social democracy, without exception, in Europe. There are communist parties that maintain a Stalinist position, which are still not open bourgeois formations, for instance in Greece and Portugal.

There was working-class resistance to neo-liberalism: the 1993 Belgian general strike, the big movements in the public sector in Britain, the movement of 1995 against the Juppé plan – a huge movement. In all of these, it was very clear that there was opposition, but the alternative, the alternative government even, was not obvious to the masses. How can we in France put forward a Socialist-Communist government as an alternative to the right in the context of the Socialist Party adapting to the situation and, in effect, giving support to the ideas of neo-liberalism? That raised in our minds the need for new workers' parties. France was different because there was an opportunity for Trotskyists, especially after the 2002 election, to create the basis of a left revolutionary party if the LO and the LCR had come together. But that was not the case in the rest of Europe.

What is the relationship of forces now? The bourgeoisie has had one of its best opportunities in history to underline the advantages of their system. They have had no real opposition from the political leaders or former leaders of the organised working class. All the main parties – from right to 'left' – have collaborated in neo-liberalism. Francis Fukuyama said that the collapse of the Berlin Wall represented the 'end of history'. He did not mean that history had ended but that the most finished form for humanity in its long historical ladder of ascent was bourgeois democracy, with the US at the centre of this idea. It is not an accident that Fukuyama has, in effect, abandoned the ideas of neo-conservatism in the last couple of months, particularly the world hegemony of US imperialism.

There are now enormous doubts and hesitations as the European bourgeoisie's project for European unity has stalled. The Bolkestein services directive has not gone through in its original form; the European constitution is blocked and stalled at the present time. The bourgeoisie will come back to this but will meet resistance. So the relationship of forces is potentially favourable to the working class. A key question is whether the subjective factor will develop in the broad sense of the term, a broad party within which Trotskyists and Marxists could participate. One of the reasons why the bourgeoisie has got away with what it has in the last 15 years is the fact that on the political and trade union planes there has been no effective check to its untrammelled rule. When there were 'bourgeois' workers' parties, the capitalists at least had to look over their shoulders before they could consider taking action against the working class because these parties, with one foot in the camp of the working class, were forced to respond to the movement from below.

This decade then is potentially a favourable period. We have a certain equilibrium now in the relationship of forces. It develops in a very contradictory way. The movement in France temporarily demoralised the bourgeoisie, there is no doubt. The European bourgeoisie is also semi-demoralised because its 'project' for Europe has not been implemented. The American ruling class jeers: 'Europe cannot compete with us, it is now just a museum.' Italy is extremely symptomatic of this.

However, the European bourgeoisie will not forever accept their second-rate status easily. They will be prepared to take action to attack the working class. Italy is one of the most important countries in Europe now. The offensive against the living standards of the working class has to be much sharper and deeper from a bourgeois point of view in Italy than is the case perhaps in other European countries. Despite the weaknesses of the leadership, the Italian working class checked up to a point some of the worst attacks that Berlusconi was proposing. So that gives a breathing space for a certain political regroupment, especially for the conscious Marxist and revolutionary forces, and the opportunity for the new generation to begin to move into action under the impact of events.

Women and civil servants - New layers involved in struggle

Russia, Eastern Europe and State Capitalism

On the question of Eastern Europe, what was the process of the counter-revolution and why was there not a serious revolutionary movement of the Russian working class?

We have written a lot of material on this. The collapse of the Soviet Union and Eastern Europe was one of the greatest setbacks for the working class and Marxists in history. It was perhaps one of the three most important events in the 20th century: 1917 and its repercussions; the end of the Second World War and the balance of forces that came out of that; and the collapse of these Stalinist regimes. The positions that Marxists took towards those events was crucial for the subsequent development of the forces of Marxism and Trotskyism.

Having previously held a perspective that it was unlikely that there would be a return to capitalism, we began to amend that position in the late 1980s. This provoked a schism in our ranks. Whereas Ted Grant and his supporters clung to the previous perspective, we, in the light of the events in Poland, said there could now be a return to capitalism. Why did we say that? Because of the world capitalist boom of the 1980s and the evident signs of economic stagnation in the Soviet Union. On the basis of a modern economy, it was no longer possible to use the bureaucratic methods of Stalinism.

The choice was between workers' democracy and a return to capitalism. If we had had forces inside Russia we may have come to a more correct conclusion about the process much earlier. What was the consciousness of the masses? In the 1980s, Solidarity was, at bottom, a searching by the Polish workers for the ideas of workers' democracy but also with pro-capitalist elements in the movement, as there were in 1956 in Hungary. But the predominant feature in the documents and congresses of Solidarity, despite its religious colouration and the cover of Catholicism, was this search for the idea of workers' democracy: accepting the planned economy but with democracy. However, the suppression of Solidarity in 1981 and Jaruzelski's rise to power (who subsequently admitted it was a mistake for him to resort to military measures and to recentralise and maintain the bureaucratically controlled economy) changed the consciousness of the Polish workers. Under the pressure of events they moved towards the right, assisted by the hierarchy of the Catholic Church. The intervention of Thatcher and George Bush senior, and the move of the bureaucracy itself towards a pro-capitalist position, laid the basis for the change in consciousness by suggesting that, while 'everything else had been tried', maybe the market was the way forward.

In Russia and in East Germany there were, at least in the first period, elements of the ideas of workers' democracy to the fore. It was not a worked-out perspective but it was there. Bob Labi wrote a book on the collapse of East Germany in 1989 in which some of these features are explained. We carried a lot of material, including an important document, on the collapse of Stalinism. Our ex-comrades disagreed with us and split away to form the Grant-Woods group. But the main reason why the elements of workers' democracy, evident at the beginning of the movement, did not develop further was because the Russian working class had been kept in the dark almost since the 1920s. They experienced the purges of the 1930s and the dark night of Stalinism afterwards, a period of about 60 years. There were flare-ups, when sections of the population, while defending the planned economy, looked towards workers' democracy. But as the 1980s developed, it was quite clear there was only a minority then who believed, understood or even had access to the ideas of workers' democracy. There was a passivity amongst certain layers, even in the factories, which our comrades reported on when they travelled to the country at the end of the 1980s. The net result was a return to capitalism by the bureaucracy, without a 'civil war'. This seems to contradict a point Trotsky once made that there could not be a class change in Russia without a civil war because this would mean that the "film of reformism would be run backwards".

Yes, that is related to the question on the purpose of the theory of state capitalism today. Trotsky said that the working class would struggle against the restoration of capitalism but they did not struggle and there was no civil war. Also, that a restoration was impossible without a counter-revolution.

As a general proposition that is correct and was valid at a certain historical stage. When Trotsky was writing, the Russian Revolution was still fresh in the minds of the proletariat. There was still a consciousness, wrote Trotsky, of the gains of the October Revolution and even a fear that if the bureaucrats were overthrown it would open the gates to bourgeois counter-revolution. Trotsky's proposition is correct as a general theoretical norm. But a theoretical norm can never completely describe reality. As Goethe once said: "Theory is grey and green is the tree of life, my friend." Lenin was fond of repeating that point. Even in relation to the transformation from feudalism to capitalism, in general, reforms prepared the way for revolution. But there were occasions when there was a deadlock. The bourgeoisie was too timid and afraid of leading the people to carry through the bourgeois-democratic revolution. Feudal layers, 'from the top', do the job of curtailing feudal elements and take the step of going over to capitalism. Engels makes the point that the Junkers, based in the large estates of Prussia, were forced to carry through the measures that laid the basis for the development of German capitalism because the bourgeoisie itself was too timid and afraid of the proletariat to take the lead, as 1848 had shown. You could also say that something similar happened in Japan and, in particular, in the aftermath of the Second World War. MacArthur actually carried through land reform from the top.

Some of Cliff's other theoretical ideas – for instance, that surplus value was created in 1928 – are just bogus. The essence of a workers' state is that many of the elements of capitalism still exist in the first period: classes, production of commodities, money, the production of value and the production of surplus value. The difference is that it becomes social, appropriated by the workers' state rather than by the individual capitalists or the capitalist class as a whole. So the idea that there was not a surplus produced in the early stages of the Russian Revolution is just wrong. But the appropriation of the surplus by the state, therefore, alters the situation; quantity turns into quality. The new society still bears the birthmarks of the previous one but it is a qualitatively different state.

There are periods in history when there is a deadlock, when the dominant class – or caste in this case – is in a blind alley and cannot take society forward. The population of the 'Soviet Union' saw the dislocation 70 years after the revolution and contrasted this to the seeming dazzling economic success of the West. The bureaucracy, the majority of it, used this to go over to capitalism. The resistance then comes when the effects of capitalism are felt by the proletariat. The fast-track return to capitalism which the Chinese have avoided, for fear of the social consequences, absolutely stunned the proletariat.

The level of poverty and unemployment in Russia in the first part of the 1990s had no precedent in history. The only comparison is the US of 1929-33 and, in real terms, Russia's was a much greater collapse. Some bourgeois economists say that Russia today has an equivalent economic power to Belgium. I think that is an underestimation of Russia's economic strength because it does not take into account oil. But the very fact that this comparison is used is a measure of the economic and industrial collapse which was accompanied by a stunning reduction in social services, education, etc. Life for millions became a struggle for a piece of bread. There seemed to be no alternative to capitalism.

When I was in Russia in 1998, never mind the early 1990s, comrades from Kazakhstan related that there was no electricity. The masses were breaking up their furniture and the doors of their houses. They had open fires in the streets in sub-zero temperatures just to keep warm. In a situation like that, particularly after being kept in the dark night of Stalinism for 60 years, how could the masses have developed the necessary consciousness to fight for workers' democracy? The CWI said, when we discussed the question of Stalinism in the past, that it would be possible once the spark ignited a mass movement, that this could overthrow the bureaucracy, even though the Trotskyists and conscious Marxist forces did not then exist in these societies. In Hungary in 1956, the masses had experienced 20 years of Horthy fascist terror, ten years of Stalinist terror, and the period of democracy was short, a very 'delicate flower' going back to Bela Kun in 1919. What democratic traditions did the Hungarian workers have? Yet when they rose in 1956, two general strikes smashed the first Russian army. The second intervention used Mongolian troops who were told they were going to fight a fascist uprising in Berlin! But the workers' councils of Hungary developed all the elements of workers' democracy: election of officials, right of recall, etc. They were ideologically very muddled – there were pro-capitalist and fascist elements in the movement – but the predominant outlook of the working class was for workers' democracy. But that was in the period when the planned economy had a certain viability. In Czechoslovakia in 1968, it was a matter of 'the human face of socialism', but there were elements of the political revolution there too, although Dubcek reflected 'liberal' national Stalinism.

Russian Stalinism was a nightmare for the Russian workers. Marx said that tradition lies on the brain of the living like an alp. This was a terrible historical experience which did not prepare the working class for the period of 1988-89. We speculated, even though we were weak, that if a revolution like Hungary broke out in Russia, only a thousand cadres would be needed to begin to build a mass party. But that proved to be utopian. In the course of a revolution the masses improvise and throw up their own organisations, and could even establish the outline of a workers' state, in the same way as the Paris Commune was the first workers' state, an anticipation of the future workers' state. But the Hungarian workers were not given sufficient time to create a party able to consolidate and spread the revolution.

It is not a question of just following the texts or phrases of Trotsky but to understand his method of analysis. After the shock which the Russian proletariat experienced, it has inevitably taken a long time for them to recover. This is the paradox of the 1990s. The area of the world in which it has been most difficult to establish viable genuine Marxist or Trotskyist forces has been in Russia, the former USSR and Eastern Europe. Why? Because of the discrediting of the official doctrine of 'Marxism', at least in the minds of the freshest elements, the youth. They were the most enthusiastic about the return to the market and the opportunities which they believed would open up, whereas the older generation, which suffered most, were the ones who retained their support for the so-called 'Communist' Party and even harked back to the planned economy. Nevertheless, the CWI has been the most successful organisation to establish a base for Trotskyism there.

In passing, Cuba could be a different situation to what happened in Russia and Eastern Europe. US imperialism has made a big mistake with the adoption of the Helms-Burton Act. It gives no section of the bureaucracy a way out. In East Germany after reunification the government said all the expropriations of land of 40 years previously could not be touched. But the Helms-Burton Act stipulates that all expropriated property in Cuba must be returned after a counter-revolution. The Mafia controlled one tenth of the assets taken over by Castro! So the heirs of Lucky Luciano and Meyer Lansky, the Mafia leaders in Cuba in the 1950s, would have the theoretical right to claim back their property. Not one section of the bureaucracy could come to an agreement with the US on this basis. If it is a question of struggle, the Cuban workers and even sections of the bureaucracy will fight. It is not a simple, straightforward issue. Whether the bureaucracy has a basis in the population is another issue entirely.

Was Trotsky right?

Bob Labi: "Each country is different. From the mid-1980s onwards, we did begin to identify the development of a pro-capitalist wing inside the bureaucracy, in the sense that the crisis in the regime had split the bureaucracy…"

Trotsky had the position that when the political revolution started there would be a split inside the bureaucracy.

Bob Labi: "It was more a crisis of the system. Peter said we underestimated the stagnation of the system. The fact was that, especially in the Soviet Union, they had problems and a section of the bureaucracy began to look quite clearly for a more capitalist way out. At that stage we identified things which had a certain similarity to, shall we say, Bukharinite developments of the late 1920s and early 1930s, not in the sense of resurrecting Bukharin's ideas but in looking towards capitalism as the way out. We identified that but we did not expect it to become the predominant wing, although it did. We did not expect that immediately. At the same time, we did not have the illusions that some had in Yeltsin when he came into conflict with Gorbachev. When Gorbachev removed Yeltsin as Moscow party boss, there were some who had illusions that perhaps Yeltsin represented that layer which was edging towards the political revolution. We were far more cautious on that. We did not have illusions in Yeltsin but we did not expect the actual movement to go in the way it did.

Obviously, if you look at Trotsky's writings of the 1930s, the main bulk is directed towards the question of either political revolution against the bureaucracy or a bourgeois counter-revolution on fascist lines, in fact, not in the pseudo-democratic form which took place. But he also gave a warning in a couple of lines in *Revolution Betrayed* where he writes that the stagnation in society was preparing 'an explosion... which may completely sweep out the results of the [1917] Revolution', and in a way that is what happened. [Page 286, New Park Publications edition, London, 1973] This was linked to the illusions in the West, which I think is an important question – not just of the higher living standards in Western Europe but also the existence of democratic rights, the fact that by the end of the 1980s in Western Europe there were only bourgeois-democratic regimes. The old military dictatorships of Greece, Spain and Portugal had gone, so the pro-capitalists could present capitalism as a democratic system. The combination of high living standards and democratic rights were attractive in comparison to the Stalinist regimes.

"In each country, there was a different development. In some countries, there was potential at different stages for a workers' movement. The discussions in Solidarity in 1980-81 were on a lower political level than the previous movements in Poland of 1956 or even in the late 1970s. Part of the reason for that was that in Hungary in 1956 and also in Poland, there was a section of workers who had struggled against the fascist regime and military dictatorships and had more of an idea of what socialism should be. There was a clearer consciousness than even in Poland in Solidarity in 1980-81, where there was much debate over what sort of society there should be. The whole question of whether there should be democratic control of the economy was an important issue in the very first congress of Solidarity. The left wing, so to speak, in Solidarity called for democratic control of the economy in a vague form, which was defeated by the more pro-capitalist elements. The Catholic Church also influenced the leadership and played a role. But each country was different.

"In East Germany, initially, the movement was not so explicitly pro-capitalist nor, in general, in favour of the reunification of Germany. But that changed, partly because the mass of workers in Germany were shocked by the living standards and higher productivity that they found in the West. They thought: what future have we got on our own? The Stalinists did attempt, in late 1989-90, to reassert control, which provoked a serious reaction. West Germany offered West German living standards. That was a lie as it turned out. But at the time, the majority of the East German population did not realise this. But the promise was: you will have a 'blooming landscape', you will live like West Germans, the East German mark will be transferred one-for-one for West German marks, which was a unique situation. It was not like what had been offered in other countries. That prepared the way for a capitalist united Germany."

In a way, the West German capitalists did not have a choice. Kohl, the German chancellor, declared that either we take the 'mark' to the East or the East will come to the mark! In other words, there would be mass emigration from the East to the West, which would have economically paralysed West Germany.

Bob Labi: "There were actually demonstrations in East Germany of workers, of East Germans marching with empty suitcases, demanding unification and saying: 'if we don't get unification, next time we'll come with full suitcases and leave.' In that sense, while each country was different, the speed of capitalist restoration in East Germany was a pace setter for the whole of Eastern Europe."

From a theoretical and historical point of view, Trotsky was correct again, I think, when he said: the bureaucracy will split into different factions and we would give critical support to that section of the bureaucracy which would defend, in their own way, the planned economy, without politically agreeing with them and we would go further than them. He wrote that, if there was an uprising against Stalin in Russia, then the masses, in the first instance, may turn to known figures like Zinoviev, for instance. Yet Zinoviev capitulated to Stalin, denied the Left Opposition and so on. But if there had been an uprising in the 1930s, the masses would have gone, to begin with, to those figures that they recognised from the heroic period of the revolution. The Trotskyists would give critical support to the wing represented by Zinoviev, Bukharin and others from the mid-1920s. Bukharin represented, paradoxically, an unconscious opening towards the market, towards capitalism. But on the question of the party regime he became critical of Stalin and his regime.

But by the 1980s, there was no wing of the bureaucracy that was prepared to defend the planned economy. Ted Grant made a mistake on this issue. The majority of the bureaucracy had reached their conclusions, empirically. Gorbachev did not start out consciously by going over to capitalism. It was a process with the problems of the economy leading to decentralisation. This did not work and then there was the opening to the market. Events got out of control – it was an uncontrolled movement. By 1989, no section of the bureaucracy, not even the organisers of the 1991 coup in

Russia, intended to go back to Stalinism. Jaruzelski, through his 1981 coup, had sought to return to a centralised, military form of Stalinism. It was unprecedented that a member of the military wing of the so-called Communist Party should organise a Stalinist counter-revolution. But within a matter of two years it was unviable. He could not maintain the position on the basis of a bureaucratic regime.

The situation in Russia was not the one analysed by Trotsky in the 1930s. How could it be? We tried to work out the issues ourselves. Marxists may sometimes get it right and sometimes all that is possible is a rough approximation. Where we are wrong, then we have to correct this on the basis of events. The CWI has done this in relation to our analysis of the different stages of the counter-revolution in Russia and Eastern Europe.

China's growth - Development in Shanghai

China

I want to ask about workers' states. Two questions about China. The first question: I read your material. I read that at your last world congress that the nature of the Chinese state is not so definite, the process is not finished, and your Swedish section, or a majority of your Swedish section, supports the idea that China is a capitalist state. But this document came out...

About five years ago.

In the last years, in the period since your last congress, have you changed your position about China, or are you staying with the position of some years ago?

Well, we are in the process of discussing this now. So, the whole question will be under review. Our position in general is that since 1978 and Deng's reforms China has been on a slow inexorable return to capitalism. There are purely capitalist sectors in China in the coastal provinces, Shanghai, in Beijing, etc. That is indisputable. If anything, that process was speeded up somewhat in the 1990s. The main reason why the Chinese Stalinists, ex-Stalinists, are hesitant in going the whole way is the fear of provoking a social explosion. It is also the reason why the rate of growth of the Chinese economy is exponential in comparison to the situation in Eastern Europe, the former Soviet Union and so on, as well as world capitalism as a whole. It is, together with the US, the economic engine of world capitalism, averaging 8-10% growth, maybe even more than that this year.

So the process is clear. But this is not a normal state. We are talking about one quarter of humankind. There are huge diversities between different parts of China, some of which are already capitalist. On the other hand, there are big sections of China in which the state sector is maintained for social reasons.

The state-organised enterprises (SOEs) still account for the majority of employment in China. On the other hand, the latest figures seem to show that the majority of wealth produced – the value, output – now comes from the private sector. But the big problem that we have is that in one month of this year we had three different reports. One said that 80% of the economy is in the private sector, another report carried in the *Financial Times* said that 25% is in the private sector, while another gave another figure. Because of the very nature of the regime, and because it is a closed society, it is very difficult to find out what is happening internally. Our position is that the China train is on the tracks and is going towards capitalism. When and at what stage it will arrive at the station is open to discussion and debate.

There is a huge state sector. There is resistance to the process of returning to capitalism, as is shown by the numbers of disputes that have broken out. The process of privatisation in agriculture has not been carried through as it has, to the same extent, in the industrial sector. All of these factors make us a bit cautious about a premature characterisation: this is now Chinese capitalism and that is the end of the matter. Elements of the Stalinist state machine still exist. There are still elements in the consciousness of the masses of support for the idea of the planned economy. There is resistance to the selling off of land. There is resistance to the closure of the SOEs, which is different and on a higher level than in Russia and Eastern Europe, where there was hardly any resistance. The Chinese bureaucracy/capitalist class is very hesitant about going too far for fear of provoking huge upheavals. We will discuss what is taking place in China between now and our congress.

However, we have general agreement about the conclusions that we should reach about the process. A revolution is being prepared in China. Trotsky always made the point that we do not think in fixed categories. Revolution and counter-revolution are both a process. He was very cautious about putting the nameplate of 'workers' state', 'non-workers' state', 'capitalist state' on a process, on unfinished processes, as he put it. We show the same caution. There are analogies, for instance, in the neo-colonial world in the 1950s, 1960s and 1970s, in particular, where large sections of industry were taken over and, to all intents and purposes, according to certain criteria, they qualified as workers' states. There was a tendency to define them as such maybe a bit prematurely.

Were Iran in 1979 and Syria workers' states?

Not Iran. But this is something that we have to look at, we have to re-examine the present situation on the basis of events. There can be periods of history when there is a deadlock, a class-economic deadlock in which the features, if you like, of both societies can exist alongside of one another. What was Gaddafi's regime, where the majority of industry was in the hands of the state? Or for that matter Egypt? We did not call them deformed workers' states. So we have to be a bit cautious from the reverse point of view in relation to China.

The question is whether it has gone from quantity to quality. Trotsky always made the point: well, you have to give a characterisation at a certain stage of a state, because from that flows the character of the revolution. Will it be a social revolution or will it be a political revolution? Will the state superstructures need to be altered? In a way, we have both tasks in China. We have in the considerable state sector demands that properly pertain to the political revolution: defence of the nation-alised property relations, for workers' control and management, election of all officials and the right of recall, and so on. In the purely capitalist sector, we demand the nationalisation or renationalisation of these sectors and their integration into a national plan, as well as workers' control and management.

An additional factor is that China itself could break up. The bureaucracy tries to give the impression that China is a homogenous whole and that one language is spoken. There might be one official language but the spoken language can be as different as Japanese and Korean. There are also regional factors: the Muslims in the North-West, Tibet, regional factors now emphasised by the economic disparity that has increased. It is as it was in Yugoslavia, where the difference between Serbia, Slovenia and Croatia on the one side, and Kosova on the other was on a level of six to one. In effect, an almost developed country and a neo-colonial one co-existed in the same state.

The same disparities exist, only more so, in China. Astonishingly, China has more poor people than the whole of Africa. On the basis of the merry-go-round of the world economy, the Chinese elite is managing to hold the situation in check. But once there is a world crisis, which could be precipitated by China, the perspectives will alter decisively.

The last point is on the consciousness of the Chinese masses. It has been thrown back so far that most groups which come into opposition to the regime seem to gravitate towards a Maoist position to begin with. Mao is associated with leading the Chinese Revolution and the advantages of the planned economy. In Eastern Europe and Russia, most of the groups of young people, in particular, did not hark back to Stalin. Pro-Stalin attitudes were to be found in the old supporters of the Communist Party but not amongst the majority of the youth. Where movements have erupted in China so far they have not been in the major industrial areas. There have been protests over village land to be handed over to speculators, and on the sell off of factories, but mostly in a scattered way. But they have not occurred in Beijing, in Shanghai or, in the main, even in Guangdong. The consciousness of the masses, it seems, is for trade union rights. The next movement may not even be like 1896 in Russia, with the big strikes in Petrograd and so on, which paved the way for 1905. It may even be a pre-1896 movement, in the sense of the masses testing their strength and gathering themselves together in the struggle for basic democratic rights, particularly on the question of independent trade unions.

Revolution in China

In our discussions, some comrades have studied and begun to look very seriously at China, which people all over the world are doing. On one side, we see the very quick development of the economy in many areas. That the development is big no one can deny. We also look at the US policy for the next century and its main rival will be China. When we began to study this question, we said we would not see the period of struggle between China and the US to become the most important capitalist power in the world. Before then, we would see a revolution in China. We are sure that before China arrives at the level of the US or near it, there will be some big conflict worldwide, not only inside China, and that clashes and problems should resolve that question before that position is reached. The second point is the level of the class struggle in China today. We have little information about the different kind of class struggles in any way: traditional class struggle in the factories, or in 'unclassical' struggles similar to those in the period of primitive accumulation, as Marx explained, but more radical and open. We have had reports of big rebellions in the rural areas against municipalities. The factor of the working class and the migrant people today and the next years will become the most important factor for the Chinese revolution and the world revolution. We have many hopes about this. Our discussion started in the last year. I would like to know what your ideas are about this and do you have a 'Third World' position? We think seriously that China will be the centre of the world. What is your opinion?

China is a major issue for world politics, for the bourgeoisie but also for the workers' movement and for Marxism. That is why the CWI has set up the Chinaworker website precisely to open up a dialogue in general with the young people and workers in China who are looking for genuine Marxist ideas.

We have to be conditional about the future. At the moment, the main axis in world politics, potentially at least, is developing between the US and China. The US, as mentioned before, has a sort of 'schizophrenic' attitude towards China. China is vital for it economically but at the same time the US fears its independent development. The US is in favour of foreign direct investment going into Guangdong, the coastal provinces and elsewhere, into the purely capitalist sectors, because it is still under the control of foreign capital.

But it also fears technology transfer to China. The US still has the edge technologically in research and development, in the application of technology. Its huge arms expenditure gives it an edge because most of the technological spin-offs come from this. It is one of the reasons why the US wants to maintain its lead, not only in arms potential but also in arms production. It is also the reason why, when Europe attempted to supply missile technology to China, the US objected. This was also partly because of the implications for Taiwan. There is an additional factor as well: the fear that a rising power 'borrows' ideas and technology from the more advanced. The issue of 'intellectual property rights' is important in the negotiations between China, Western Europe and the US. Even Merkel, the German Chancellor, when she visited China recently, gave a warning to the Chinese regime: it should not use 'pirate' technology from the US and Western Europe.

What they are afraid of is that while, at the moment, China is dependent on foreign direct investment, and that will continue for a time, it will nevertheless develop indigenous industry. The scale of this borrowing will dwarf what Japan was able to do in electronics in the 1970s and 1980s. Already, there is quite a high level of technology in China in some sectors. There is also a huge development in student numbers but at this stage there is not the same quality of education which exists in the US. Technology, at the moment, is more extensive than intensive in the development of new products, etc. But just as, in the 1980s, Hollywood made movies about the Japanese 'threat' so, in the modern era, in this century, China is the new threat.

The difference between Japan and China is that Japan was disarmed at the end of the Second World War. It is now a junior policeman, or potential policeman, for US imperialism in the Asian theatre in particular. But China has huge armed forces. There is the Peoples' Liberation Army but also the development of China's navy. The building of a navy flows from trade. There is a new scramble for Africa taking place in which China has made huge gains, in Angola, Mozambique and Nigeria, for example. There are the relations with Pakistan where they have facilities in Baluchistan. There are trade relations with Venezuela, Cuba, Brazil and Latin America.

The geopolitical impact of China is colossal and, at the moment, the American ruling class is in a halfway house. Do they see China as a 'strategic partner' or a 'strategic rival'? There are elements of both in their current position. Will the USA, with only 5% of the world's population and a big part of the resources of the planet and the dominant power, give up without a fight against a population of 1.2 billion? It is highly unlikely. There are now voices within the American establishment, particularly in the universities and amongst sinologists, who are saying that China is already a threat to the US and it has to block the transfer of technology to China. That could happen, especially if there is a world economic recession. If China is hemmed in by this situation there could be the scenario you mentioned for a revolution. It could happen anyway, whether there is an increase in the economy or not. Revolution flows not just from a collapse or from an increase in the economy. If the economy continues to go ahead but the change from one era to another is unable to absorb the unemployed and the 200 million migrant workers, there could be explosions in Shanghai, Beijing and in some of the colossal urban areas. What the outcome of that will be is not possible to say at this stage.

So perspectives on China are conditional on a whole number of factors, not least of which is the movement that will take place of the working class in the US, the movements in Latin America and the rest of Asia, and not least in Europe. I do not think that this is a 'third worldist' position. The USFI once had the theory that the 'epicentres' of the world revolution were no longer in Europe but in the 'Third World'. Cuba became the epicentre, then Vietnam, of the world revolution. We always disputed that. We saw the working class in the metropolitan countries, the 'heavy battalions' of the working class, as decisive. But potentially, the most powerful industrial proletariat in the world is developing now in China. China has the elements of the Third World and the First World. Because of that, China and its working class are destined to play in this new era, potentially, a most important role in the development of the revolution worldwide.

One thing is absolutely certain. If there is a break in the situation of capitalism in one important country or a continent where the working class plays the main role, and that must be emphasised, that could trigger a world upheaval. There could also be a break with capitalism in an underdeveloped country in which the country is largely peasant and not proletarian. It will have an effect like Cuba but it would not have the effect of the Russian Revolution, the 'ten days that shook the world'. The reason for that is not just the size of Russia but the pronounced role of the proletariat, with soviets, internationalism and the key role of the working class. If in Europe now one or two countries break with capitalism and it encompasses the whole of Europe, which it will once it starts, that would have world repercussions. It would have an immediate effect on China, because the European working class would appeal to the Chinese working class to demand trade union rights, democratic rights and so on. On the other hand, the Chinese masses could rise and could develop powerful independent workers' organisations without overthrowing the regime.

That is why I mentioned Russia in 1896 and 1905, which were anticipations of the Russian Revolution. 1896 was the first blooding and fusing of the working class as a class. In 1905 the working class reached out for power but the peasants were not ready. 1917 was a combination of the proletarian revolution and the second edition of the Peasant War, as Marx put it.

History – Militant and the CWI

Could you sum up the history, firstly, of Militant and, secondly, of the CWI? What were the major landmarks?

Militant did not drop from the sky. We trace our antecedents back to the Revolutionary Communist Party in Britain and, of course, to Trotsky's International Left Opposition. My generation joined in the early 1960s, others later. We began Militant in 1964 when we were still together with another group and the official section of the USFI in Britain. But we were always in opposition to the USFI leadership on a range of questions. On the question of Europe and whether it could be unified on a capitalist basis; on the issue of the economic upswing in which Ernest Mandel leaned towards a 'neo-Keynesian' type of position; on the colonial revolution as it was then – the revolution in the colonial world; on the attitude towards the left within the Labour Party, in which they had a position of 'deep entrism', hiding their ideas. At the world congress of the USFI in 1965, we were effectively expelled from the USFI.

Militant was started in 1964 when a new generation came into our ranks. At the outset we were few in number. The anti-war movement and the anti-nuclear weapons movement called the Campaign for Nuclear Disarmament (CND) was very big in Britain in 1959-60. The marches to Aldermaston, the research headquarters for nuclear weapons production, were important. Then the big apprentices' strikes took place, the strikes of young workers in the engineering industry in 1960 and 1964. A number of comrades came to Trotskyism through the youth wing of the Labour Party.

We met up with an older generation of Trotskyists, such as Ted Grant, Jimmy Deane, Arthur Deane and so on. In the early 1960s, after a short period, we collaborated with the Cliff group, today's SWP, in a journal called *Young Guard*, within the youth wing of the Labour Party. We found that we were not compatible in approach, so we founded Militant in 1964. This was not an ideal name. We have had more discussion on the names for the papers than any other issue. But in time, all names become synonymous with a definite trend and a body of ideas.

We decided to call ourselves Militant. We had a subhead, 'For Labour and Youth'. And that was deliberate because we believed the Labour Party then was the place to be. The Labour Party was a bourgeois workers' party with a leadership which had always been bourgeois. But the base of the party was the trade unions, the organised working class. The first issue of the paper was an eight-page monthly. We had no full-timers before we started building Militant. I became the first full-timer.

How many people?

We had about 40 comrades nationally, a combination of an older generation and young people. The youth came to the fore while most of the older generation dropped away, although there were some notable exceptions. It was predominantly a youth organisation actually, in the first period. And when I say youth, I'm talking about people of 18-21. I became a Trotskyist when I was 18. The overwhelming majority were young people. Some of our comrades were no more than 14 or 15 and they have stayed the course.

We rooted ourselves in the Labour Party. We were fortunate in the sense that the Young Socialists were formed in 1960 and renamed as the Labour Party Young Socialists (LPYS) from 1964. The SWP/IST (the Cliff group) left the Labour Party in the mid-1960s. The Gerry Healy group left or were expelled earlier because of the methods that they used. So, in a way, we had a clear field. But we were small. We did not have anybody on the National Committee of the LPYS initially. Then one comrade from Scotland was elected, and then we won another comrade already on the National Committee. By 1970, we had won a majority on the LPYS National Committee. Eventually, we won all the regional places on the National Committee. This was achieved by consistent, patient work but also through argument and a scrupulously democratic attitude and comradely approach in discussion.

We also worked within the Labour Party itself, the adult party, and we always had a base in the trade unions. Our organisation always has been, and always will be, predominantly a working-class organisation, although with a very good layer of students, young intellectuals who have broken from capitalism, some who have broken from their bourgeois or petty-bourgeois background and put themselves on the standpoint of the proletariat. It was never a problem about people coming in from different backgrounds because of the process of integration into our organisation of those coming from a different social milieu than the working class.

We built up our position, very slowly. We decided we could not cover everything. If you aim at the sky, you will always score a bull's-eye but be diffuse. So if you have 40 people you concentrate them in a specific field, the most important arena where you can make gains. Hence, in Italy it does not make much difference where you would first win adherents to Marxist ideas. It is a question of winning a base, developing and educating them, and then deciding where you would deploy those forces. In Britain it did not really make all that much difference to begin with whether it was in the Labour Party or outside the Labour Party. We won people wherever we could and then, to use a military term, it was all forces at the point of attack. So we were in the LPYS and we won a majority. We then had an echo of this within the Labour Party.

In the 1970s there was tremendous upheaval in society. We went from a monthly paper to a fortnightly paper. We bought our own printing press. We collected money from every comrade and sympathiser. We were very self-sacrificing. We made demands on ourselves and others, and still do. If people have got a good job they pay a high proportion of their salary to our organisation. We make no secret of that. If someone is unemployed they make a sacrifice which is smaller but equivalent and as valued as somebody who is in a good job. We built up our resources. As well as the printing press we acquired small premises in which we printed the paper. I was the only full-timer. I was taken on as a full-timer when I was 20. I was also the general secretary. We started a fortnightly paper. Then we went over to a weekly, expanded our press and increased the number of full-timers. We talked about producing the paper two or three times a week, and did occasionally. We were talking, at one stage, about producing a daily paper. But we always had the attitude that the production of the paper was not an end in itself, it was a means to an end. It was a lever to the other political work that we were doing.

We eventually built up Militant to a sizeable organisation in the 1970s, coming to national prominence in about 1976 over the question of the youth officer of the Labour Party. One of our comrades, Andy Bevan, was selected to become the youth officer of the Labour Party although he was a well-known Marxist and Trotskyist. The capitalist press, backed by the right wing of the Labour Party and officials, tried to get him sacked. We defeated that attack. We were seen by Labour members as 'good young people' who were doing a good job, the Labour Party was a 'broad church' and should accept different trends and so on. Remember, the Labour Party since the 1920s has never been like the Rifondazione Comunista (RC) in Italy, accepting official tendencies. You could organise a newspaper, a group of like-minded 'friends', but you could not officially be in an organisation, although the right wing was organised and the Labour machine was their organisation.

We methodically developed our position, having a big effect on the Labour Party conference in the late 1970s. In 1978, we defeated the national leadership of the Labour Party on the key question of the 'Social Contract'. This was an agreement between the official trade union leaders and the Labour government to hold down wages. A resolution to the Labour Party conference was moved by one of our comrades, which effectively opened the door for the unions to break the Social Contract. The trade unions took the resolution as a signal to come out of the Social Contract which, in turn, led to the so-called 'winter of discontent'. The low-paid public-sector workers went on strike, which brought the working class into head-on collision with the government. That led to the defeat of the Labour government of 1979 and the coming to power of Thatcher.

Britain in the 1980s

I will not go fully into the political background, but that opened up an entirely different situation in Britain. The decade of the 1980s was most important for genuine Marxism, Trotskyism, in Britain. Thatcher was the whip of the counter-revolution. In Liverpool we had built up a powerful position within the Labour Party. We were a minority on the City Council Labour group but we convinced the Labour group to confront Thatcher on the issue of a 'needs budget'. The government had taken £60m away. We did not come to power in the local council to do as, I believe, in Italy the RC and the DS, do, that is, to administer neo-liberal reforms in a 'mild way' claiming to 'mitigate' the effects. We said no, we would not carry through any cuts in council services or increase the rates – a local property tax which affected the lower middle class and workers. We would declare a 'needs budget' with a deficit and demand that the extra amount for spending should come from the government. This was an 'illegal budget'. The government must give back to Liverpool £70m it had stolen from the city.

In order to force them to do that, a mass mobilisation was necessary. Labour won control of the city council in 1983 with a huge majority and increased it in 1984. We organised two general strikes in Liverpool and in 1984 produced an illegal budget which, technically, made the councillors liable to be fined by the government. To cut a long story short, Thatcher retreated in 1984 because the miners' strike was taking place at that stage as well. She made financial concessions to Liverpool. We and the Liverpool workers won a victory. But the miners were defeated in 1985. Thatcher came back and penalised the council for its 1985 budget. She would not have been able to get away with this without the support of the right-wing leaders of the trade unions and, particularly, of Neil Kinnock, the then leader of the Labour Party.

I want to stress that the number of councillors who were Militant, that is, members of the Militant Tendency, as we called ourselves then, were always a minority. We did not have a majority of the councillors. We had a powerful position in the unions as well and an important presence in the Labour Party. But, because we had a worked-out strategy, the majority of the councillors, the left, and even some who formally stood on the right, went along with our strategy and saw no alternative. We mobilised from below to put pressure on those who wavered.

The government was defeated in Liverpool in 1984 but a witch-hunt had already started, a vicious attack to drive us out of the Labour Party, orchestrated by the bourgeoisie and taken up by the rightwing of the Labour Party. Clare Doyle, myself, Keith Dickinson, Ted Grant and Lynn Walsh who were on the Militant Editorial Board, the 'official' leadership of Militant, were expelled in a blaze of publicity. We were all over the television, radio and the press. Kinnock then attacked the Liverpool councillors in 1985-86. We describe these events in our book: *Liverpool – A City that Dared to Fight*. After the Editorial Board was expelled in 1983, they then came for the Militant leaders of the Liverpool struggle in 1985-86 and a number were expelled. The Labour Party in that city became empty.

We decided when Thatcher was re-elected in 1987 to launch the struggle against the poll tax, which was very successful despite the fact that the official Labour and trade union leadership peeled away and abandoned the fight. That resulted in the mass demonstration, the so-called 'riot', in Trafalgar Square in 1990. But the issue that buried the poll tax was the decision of 18 million people to refuse to pay it. This paralysed the collection of the tax and forced Thatcher onto the back foot. Her own MPs revolted and she was removed as prime minister.

In the late 1980s, we had 8,000 members, even though our leadership had been expelled from the Labour Party. We made some mistakes at the time when we were expelled. We should have organised an independent party then.

What was the circulation of the paper?

It varied, but at one stage it was between 15,000 and 20,000 per weekly issue. The readership was much larger than this because the paper would be passed on to friends, acquaintances and workmates. On the big poll tax demonstration of 1990, we sold 10,000 copies of the paper. You could not go anywhere without seeing sellers of the Militant. There was one famous occasion when there was a television crew making a drama programme about a strike. Some of the actors were acting out the 'strike' in a street. One of our comrades came across them, went up to the actors and tried to sell them a copy of the Militant because he thought it was a real strike! In the miners' strike we were an important left force. Arthur Scargill approached us for a bloc in the course of the miners' strike. We sent several of our comrades all over the world during the miners' strike: to South Africa, Europe and so on, alongside other miners, to raise support and solidarity.

After the poll tax struggle, there was no real life in the Labour Party. Its youth wing had been closed down and it was not possible to work as before. We launched an independent organisation. At the time, we saw this as a temporary tactic. With Kinnock in control and steadily moving to the right, and as a consequence of the Labour Party emptying out, we went outside of the Labour Party to have more effect. At the same time, we also said we would be prepared to rejoin the Labour Party if it changed. It was not really on this issue but on other issues, organisational questions, that Ted Grant and his supporters decided to organise a faction. But they moved on to other issues and were roundly defeated. At our special national conference in October 1991 of about 800 people, held in the North of England, they got 7% of the vote! They then decided that they would collect money separately for their group and subsequently formed their own separate organisation.

We then decided to continue with the independent tactic. The Labour Party became more and more empty. In the 1990s and since, because we changed our tactics, we were successful in a difficult period in retaining and building our forces. We decided to stand independently for local councils and for parliament. Britain has a much more difficult electoral system for minority parties than exists elsewhere in Europe. It is 'first-past-the-post', so a party has to get a huge number of votes to get into parliament. We now have seven councillors in England. Internationally, we have nine councillors in Germany, eight in Sweden, one in Australia, one in Sri Lanka, four in Ireland and a bloc in Pakistan.

The transitional approach

Many of the far left in Italy say that in Britain, and also in Italy, the CWI has some opportunistic positions. The first opportunistic position was about the question of the nation state and the revolution. Your comrades in Italy, in *Falce Martello*, **at the time, stated in their material, many times, that it is possible for a peaceful transition to socialism to take place. They took Engels's statement on the case of civil war in France and used this.**

The second was that in England you never spoke against the monarchy because the mass of the people have sympathy for the monarchy. Then there is the question of women and gays and minorities. You had old ideas about the level of the consciousness of the working class, about the prejudices of the working class about gays, about feminism and so on. You did not actively support feminism or gay rights. This is what was talked about in the Italian far left. It was how we thought of Militant in Britain. Still today, they continue to say that entrism is the strategy for the revolution. Of course, it is possible some

kind of independent force in some countries will develop, but the general line is 'entrism' because we will have a real revolutionary party only on the eve of revolution. But do you think it is a tactic or a strategic position? In many of Ted Grant's articles and documents you have the impression that it is strategy.

On the last point, I think that it is undoubtedly true, that Ted Grant not only considered it a strategic position but a 'principled' position. Any deviation from that was a 'denial' of a correct approach. We approach the question of the state in a transitional fashion, taking into account the consciousness of the working class, especially in the older industrial countries such as Britain. It would be posed somewhat differently in the neo-colonial world or, for instance, in Argentina in the 1970s or the 1980s, and perhaps in Italy with its 'communist' tradition. However, we put forward a transitional programme in the same way that Lenin and Trotsky did on the issue of the state.

The October Russian Revolution took place under a 'defensive' slogan, support for the Second Congress of Soviets in an armed demonstration. On the eve of the revolution, the Mensheviks, the Social Revolutionaries as well as the bourgeoisie were accusing the Bolsheviks of organising for an insurrection. Trotsky denied that. He said the workers were going out into the streets, yes in an armed demonstration, but as a defensive measure against the counter-revolution. In general, that is the way the working class and the labour movement have approached the question of force, peaceful or violent change.

Let me give you a typical example of the way that this would come up in a conversation with a worker in Britain. We were working in the Labour Party, a reformist milieu. But it had a clause in its constitution – Clause Four, Part Four – which stood for the nationalisation of the commanding heights of the economy. That clause was a reflection of the pressure of the Russian Revolution on the Labour Party in the aftermath of 1917. Blair eliminated it in 1995. That and other measures were the signal for the liquidation of the Labour Party as a workers' party. But when it was a workers' party at the bottom, we put forward transitional demands, within the party and outside, following the example of the Bolsheviks. Their slogan was for 'bread, peace and land', and everything that flowed from this. It was a combination of events and correct slogans at each stage that led to the idea of the Russian Revolution.

However, we were in a non-revolutionary period – a radicalised period, but not a revolutionary or pre-revolutionary situation, not even the situation of Italy of the 1970s. We were working in the Labour Party for the reasons I have explained before, and we put forward demands on housing, education and social services. We also put forward the demand that a Labour government should take over, using language that could be understood by workers, the 250 monopolies which controlled 80-85% of the economy, with compensation only on the basis of proven need. In other words, not complete expropriation, which I will explain. We advocated a socialist plan of production to be drawn up by the working class, trade unionists, housewives, small-business people and so on through committees that would control this plan.

That was our basic propaganda, our transitional approach. We would go to meetings, Labour Party or trade union meetings. Sometimes, these were big meetings. We would say: this is our programme for the future. You would get some of the ultra-lefts who would stand up and say: 'You are absolutely wrong, Trotsky was in favour of soviets, you should be putting forward soviets at this stage; it is to reinforce workers' illusions to think that we should work through parliament.' They were childish arguments. We had to point out to them that the majority of the population, including the working class, have illusions in bourgeois democracy and parliament, and we cannot eliminate those illusions through propaganda alone. A combination of arguments, put forward skilfully, and the experience of the working class will teach them to embrace alternative socialist and Marxist ideas.

The Bolsheviks did not even abandon the slogan of the Constituent Assembly until after the Russian Revolution, because Lenin was always worried about a retreat if the revolution stalled. The Constituent Assembly was only dissolved when the masses had established the alternative of soviet power, the soviet government. It shows the care with which Lenin and Trotsky approached the outlook of the working class and the popular masses.

How do we break the illusions of the working class on the question of bourgeois 'democracy'? Workers would ask: if a government came in and introduced the measures Militant advocates for parliament, is the ruling class going to just accept this? It would organise a military conspiracy. We would say, we agree with you. But in that situation and in the situation leading up to it, we would demand that the trade unions and working-class parties prepare the working class in defence of any radical measures which were to be introduced. We would give them examples, of what happened in Chile. There was the parliamentary struggle of Allende and the extra-parliamentary activity of the masses for arms. The same happened in the Spanish Revolution.

All of these points we brought out. Not in a little room. I am talking about meetings and rallies of hundreds and sometimes thousands of people, and on TV and radio. We would say: we are not pacifists, we will defend the right to strike, freedom of assembly, etc, with force of arms if necessary, if they are threatened by reaction or fascism. But so would, we hope, all workers and the left leaders in particular. We are not at the stage which the ultra-lefts have come here to talk about.

Then the argument would arise: are you going to compensate the capitalists for fleecing the workers? Trotsky raises this point in a discussion on the transitional programme. He said: "We would even be prepared to buy the capitalists out, we are not theoretically opposed to that." So we put forward the idea of compensation to small shareholders on the basis of proven need. We would not fully compensate the big capitalists and the huge stockholders, but perhaps the small men and women. Bourgeois propaganda on this issue invariably taunts: 'If the big companies are taken over what about the investment of the little man with a few shares?' We would compensate them. But not the big shareholders, not the billionaires.

Then the question is posed of what kind of state are you aiming for? Do you think that parliament will be retained? Trotsky theoretically raised that you would not necessarily replace 'parliament', the building, *per se*. But the basis upon which it would be constituted would be radically changed. The way we formulate it – for a socialist plan of production, drawn up by committees of workers, trade unionists, shop stewards and so on – is a popularised form of what are, strictly speaking, workers' councils or 'soviets'. Our ultra-left friends could not see it but we did it in such a way that the average worker could grasp what we were driving at.

On a general theoretical level, we defend the ideas of Marx on the character of the state in his writings on the Paris Commune, of Lenin at the time of the Russian Revolution and of Trotsky. We have never, ever, used the quote of Engels in the introduction to the *Class Struggles in France* to argue that 'peaceful change' is the only option. In fact, we argued exactly the opposite. It was Kautsky and Co who falsified the circumstances and intention of Engels in that particular quote.

Bob Labi: "We had polemics against the CP on that."

We said: we are not pacifists, read our material, we will fight, but so will ordinary trade unionists. We would hope that Tony Benn and Jack Jones (leader of the Transport and General Workers' Union in the 1970s who went through the Spanish Civil War), would be alongside us fighting to defend the right to vote, the right to strike and freedom of assembly. With this approach, no Labour leader could accuse us of being 'wild men with knives between their teeth', to assert, 'they are mad, they just want an armed confrontation, they want civil war'. Marxists and Trotskyists have to overcome the arguments of our opponents who imply that we want an 'immediate armed insurrection'. That is why we need a transitional approach.

On the question: can it be done peacefully? The Russian Revolution was carried through, initially, peacefully. The storming of the Winter Palace; how many people were killed? A handful. The violence came afterwards from the bourgeoisie in the civil war.

On the state, in our theoretical journal and special pamphlets we explain our position at length and in detail. We have also featured explanations of the state in our weekly paper. On the question of a peaceful transition, would you say to workers, 'we want violence, we want civil war'? We would argue that we want to carry through a change through winning a majority, a democratic majority. In the Russian Revolution there was a democratic vote in the soviets; the Bolsheviks took power. No party was illegalised in the first period except the Black Hundred fascists. The Bolsheviks only banned other parties after they had taken up arms to overthrow the government.

Are we in favour of multi-party democracy? We answer, yes, and that includes the right to exist for the Tory party. In Italy, you would have to say the bourgeois-democratic parties have the same right. We are not in favour of granting the same rights to outright fascists. We would illegalise them. The open fascists want to destroy democratic rights, including the working-class movement. But as far as the other bourgeois parties are concerned, they would be able to participate in elections. A democratic, workers' state would have nothing to fear from them. In the Russian Revolution, the Mensheviks were not illegalised, the Bolsheviks did not close down the Social Revolutionaries. In fact, initially they went into a coalition with the Left Social Revolutionaries. But when they resorted to an uprising against democratic workers' power, then the Bolsheviks had no choice but to ban them. But it was seen as a temporary measure. Once the civil war was over, soviet democracy could be restored, the Bolsheviks reasoned. That proved to be impossible in a divided, culturally deprived society for a number of reasons. The same measures would not be necessary in a culturally, economically advanced and developed society.

If in Britain, the mobilisation of the overwhelming power of the working class could draw in the middle class, you could not then theoretically rule out that you could get a majority workers' socialist government to carry through the expropriation of the capitalists, backed up by mass support outside of parliament. In relation to the US, Marx, in the 19th century, did not theoretically rule out peaceful change because of the weakness of the standing army then. And this was the man who wrote about the capitalist state as the "armed bodies of men and their material appendages". Of course, the situation of the US has changed fundamentally since then. The US is now one of the most militarised societies in the world.

History has shown that a privileged class, group or caste will not give up its wealth and power without a fight, utilising if it can the most ruthless and, if necessary, violent means. Look what happened in Spain in 1936 and in Chile in 1972-73. If Allende had prepared the working class properly, instead of prevaricating, the outcome could have been different. He took over 25% of industry. Then, when the counter-revolution mobilised in June 1973 with the attempted coup, the workers responded by going into the factories and took over 40% of industry. They saw that the military coup was coming and demanded arms, which were refused by Allende.

In the Portuguese Revolution, when Spinola attempted his coup in March 1975, the masses responded and the government was forced to take over 70% of the industry. Then they stopped halfway. But with that power and a mass revolutionary party, they could have established such an impregnable position that the resistance of the ruling class would have been completely ineffectual. It cannot be ruled out, but it is not likely, that socialist change would be peaceful, as Chile has shown, as Spain has shown.

This is a transitional approach which leads the average worker from demanding reforms to the idea of the need for the socialist transformation. If you baldly demand the socialist revolution, soviets and the rest, you will come up against a brick wall in Britain but also in Italy at this stage.

On the issue of a republic for Britain, in our programme we call for reforms in housing, education, social services, 'take over the 250 monopolies', a state monopoly of foreign trade, but also for the abolition of the monarchy and the House of Lords. The monarchy is not just there for decorative purposes in Britain. Theoretically, every British government is appointed by the monarch and can be undemocratically dismissed without an election. The capitalist class could use the monarchy to achieve this, as it did in Australia in 1975. We are against presidencies in general just like we are against monarchs or the House of Lords. We stand in favour of the abolition, not the replacement, of the monarchy and the House of Lords.

Gays and women

On the question of gays, we never supported or fostered anti-gay prejudices. What is true is that there were some comrades who had a very crude position. They would repeat Engels's position in *Origins of the Family* condemning gay love in ancient Greece. That position of Engels has been used by some of the gay groups against Marxist ideas today. Marx and Engels were products of their time and the prejudices that existed, not of the situation which exists today or the present position of

Marxism. There was an initial reluctance of Militant to take up this issue. But we never justified the repression of gays. We never took the position of Castro or any such leader or organisation. When resolutions came up at the Young Socialist conferences, which we influenced, and elsewhere, the attitude of some was: 'well, it is not important, we will give support to it, but it will not be a major issue as far as we are concerned.' That is not the case today. We have comrades, you can see by our material, comrades in the leadership and so on, who are openly gay.

Prejudices against feminism? No, that is just not true. We are against the divisions fostered by petty-bourgeois and bourgeois feminism. So are most working-class women. They greeted the women's movement of the 1960s amongst other things because it opened the door for working-class women. We support the demands of women, it is a vital issue. In fact, some of the gains made in the past are under attack through advertising, the commodification of sex and so on.

We do not agree with some artificial demands for all-women shortlists for labour movement officials. The British working class has had experience of bourgeois 'feminism' in the form of Thatcher. Our comrades are socialist feminists, but we are not just going to go along with everything the bourgeois or petty-bourgeois feminists put forward. The USFI, particularly the American SWP, we felt, emphasised the question of gays, women and racism, while not giving sufficient emphasis to work in the trade unions and in the working class as a whole.

The organisation which was most successful in attracting, winning and integrating women, particularly working-class women but women in general, into the party and into leading positions in the party, was Militant and the Socialist Party. The Executive Committee of the England and Wales section is made up of a majority of women. They are not there just because they are women. They are there on merit, on their ability. And then there is the Campaign Against Domestic Violence (CADV) which we set up.

We had more effect on this than the organisations that are critical of us for not having sufficient concentration on women's issues. They talk a good fight but on the CADV we had a huge effect. We set up this campaign and got significant support from the trade unions. This had a lasting effect in the trade unions and in the workplaces.

The Labour Party

On 'entrism', this arose from the police-type regimes which existed in social democratic and Stalinist parties in the past. Marxists were not allowed to put forward and campaign for their ideas. That is not the case today in the new open period following the discrediting of bureaucratic and Stalinist methods. Also, this was perceived by Trotsky as a short-term tactic. An incapacity to heed Trotsky's advice in the 1930s in Spain or to use the tactic correctly wrecked the revolution. The socialist youth under Largo Caballero had openly appealed to Juan Andrade and Andres Nin: 'Come into the young socialists, take us over, you are the best theoreticians in Spain.' They refused but the Stalinists did not make that mistake. Santiago Carrillo was won over by the Stalinists. (This is detailed in the latest book by Anthony Beevor on the Spanish Civil War.) The Stalinists, who were weaker than the Trotskyists in Catalonia at the beginning, as a result of their entry and other factors, took over the socialist youth and large sections of the Socialist Party. In fact, Caballero came into collision with them. That particular tactical blunder, and the inadequacies politically of the POUM leadership, helped to wreck the revolution.

Today, the classical ideas of Trotsky on work in the 'traditional' organisations are not applicable. Marxists and Trotskyists sometimes openly adhere to broad formations, which are in ferment, where there is the right to put forward your point of view and to campaign for your programme in a friendly, comradely way inside the party itself. Unfortunately, in the 'long winter sleep', historically, during the boom of 1950-75, Marxists were reduced to a handful in Britain and also Italy. The Communist Party in Italy was a solid Stalinist monolith. The Socialist Party had certain openings, but was not even like the British Labour Party. It was a petty-bourgeois formation in large part, but at certain stages had more radical political features as well. But there were limited possibilities for Marxists to gain support when capitalism was going ahead and reformism was strong.

People like Ted Grant made a mistake in entering the Labour Party in 1948-49. He originally opposed going into the Labour Party then but, when he was defeated and had very small forces, he tried to rationalise it by saying that Marxism could make no progress either inside or outside of the Labour Party. It is not an active Marxist approach, it is contemplative. It is a quietist attitude which does not take a dynamic approach towards the possibilities for Marxism at each stage. The best tactic for Trotskyists in that period of the 1950s would have been to work independently, which Gerry Healy and his party did, although their methods were reprehensible. They largely concentrated in industry and won some militants. Then, at a later stage, when the Labour Party was radicalised and filled out, they entered the Labour Party and were initially more successful than the Grant group.

Ted Grant's perception was based on the fact that the mass communist parties created in Western Europe came from the old organisations of the proletariat, from splits in the old organisations. This occurred in Italy after the September 1920 days and the split in the Socialist Party, when a mass Communist Party was created. In Germany there was the split of 1917, then the split of the USPD, with Zinoviev going to Berlin in 1920 and speaking in German for about five hours in Halle. He won over hundreds of thousands of members of the USPD to the new Communist Party, bringing with them many daily newspapers! The same in France, with the Tours Socialist Party Congress, when the majority of the active worker members came over to the Communist International. But that was against the background of the Russian Revolution and the authority of the Communist International, when these were traditional organisations without the police-type atmosphere that developed within the Labour Party in Britain in response to the Russian Revolution. Lenin told the young Communist Party of Great Britain to work in the Labour Party and Trotsky even raised the theoretical possibility that the CP could take over and become like the Independent Labour Party, with 30,000 members, and in effect control the Labour Party. So out of this reformist or centrist milieu, there would be a revolutionary kernel, from which would develop a mass Communist Party at a certain stage. It was a correct idea and correct for us to think of that, but history has developed in a different way.

I made many speeches in the past in which I said, 'no matter what happens, we will remain in the Labour Party'. We argued against premature splits from the Labour Party, against ultra-lefts who criticised our work from a sectarian point of view. But an almost automatist perspective developed – 'we have 2,000 people now, we will be 4,000 in two years time, 8,000 soon after and then tens of thousands'. But it did not take account of the ruptures and the sharp, abrupt changes in the situation, the most important of which was the collapse of Stalinism and the effects this had in demoralising and emptying the former 'traditional' parties.

Ted Grant's followers and their co-thinkers internationally are stuck on one partic-ular tactic. It is like a golfer using only one club instead of a whole bag full! Tactics depend upon the objective situation. For us to have remained in the Labour Party in the 1990s and today would have tolled the death knell for us. In passing, I do not dispute that there are still opportunities for Marxists in the RC but they are not the only possibilities in Italy. What about the radicalised youth who are repelled from the RC? It is a fossilised view of Marxism to just have one approach of this particu-lar character. We have a variety of tactics.

We are part of the Socialist Party in the Netherlands, which has moved towards the right recently. We also work in the WASG, as you are aware, in Germany. But in other situations where there is no, even small, party which offers the opportunities and the possibilities of creating the basis for a larger formation in the working class, we pursue an independent tactic. This has been very successful on a principled, Marxist basis. For instance, our comrades in the Socialist Party in Ireland have four councillors, but also, importantly, we have Joe Higgins who is an MP, a very effective one.

If, for argument's sake, in the future the right wing is vomited out of the Labour Party and the left takes over, as happened in France with the eviction of the neo-socialists from the Socialist Party in 1934 (the Socialist Party swung over to a centrist position), in that situation, we would reconsider our approach. We have to be flexible, but we also have to see the opportunities that are developing for extending the bases of Marxism and Trotskyism today. The development of a mass party or a sizeable, Marxist revolutionary organisation is not one act or one event. It is a series of opportunities which can present themselves but they must be seized. It is an art to work out what to do in those situations, to intervene, to extend the influence and support for Marxism. Those comrades who argue you just have to maintain one tactic will find that history passes them by.

Another question is the history of the International.

This is a large subject. I have written a book on it and even that only deals in a very schematic fashion with the main points. Even when we only had members in Britain, we always considered ourselves internationalists, for obvious reasons. Capitalism is a world system and the opposition to it must be organised on international lines. The tendency is there now for the trade unions to do that, to come together across the national boundaries of Europe, which we support. But the same applies from the point of view of the working class and Marxism. That is why Marx formed the First International. We have gone over the experience of the Second International, the Third, and Trotsky's idea of the Fourth International, which still retains its validity as an idea. Putting it into practice in a mass sense has not been brought to fruition because of a combination of objective difficulties and subjective mistakes that were made by many of those leaders who adhered to Trotsky's ideas. We were always looking for international supporters.

Originally, most of them internationally came through the Labour Party Young Socialists or, accidentally, through meeting different comrades. By the time of the early 1970s, we had developed a position where we had a number of points of support internationally. A comrade who worked with us in Britain went back to Northern Ireland on the eve of the events of 1969. I went there, we had discussions with some people and won them over. That was supplemented by young Irish comrades, such as Peter Hadden, won here in Britain at Sussex University, who then went back to Ireland. That is how we established the Irish section in Northern

Ireland, but also in the South. Later on, people like Joe Higgins, the present Socialist Party MP in the Irish parliament, came along. We have a very strong position now in the South of Ireland and also in the North.

We also had a base in Sweden and we had made contacts in Sri Lanka as a result of visits which we made. We had established different points of support but it was not any kind of coherent international organisation. We only decided to set up an international organisation in 1974, in a pub in London – a bit like Karl Marx and Friedrich Engels did in the 19th century. We did not want to form an organisation and claim that we were *The* International, which is why we took the name 'Committee for a Workers' International'. Most of our recruits and our support, including young people, came through our work within the traditional organisations, which were viable at that stage. Visits were made to people in Italy, Spain and so on. In Spain, for instance, we built through a comrade who visited the Young Socialist conference here. I had discussions with him initially. Bob Labi made contact with Nigerian comrades. From that we developed the position in Nigeria. Tony Saunois built our position in Latin America, Clare Doyle and Rob Jones in Russia and so on.

However, we were almost hidden because we were working inside the 'traditional organisations', and the right wing of the British Labour Party and the bureaucracies of other parties, while they feared us organising on a national scale, were apoplectic about our international connections. Because of that we lost opportunities to establish ourselves in the consciousness of workers and revolutionaries internationally who were searching for an international organisation. So we were not really known to the more advanced layers of the working class in many parts of the world, although Militant was known. We did not even publicise the material of the CWI; it was largely internal material which was amended for public use. But with the break from Grant and his group in 1991/92, we decided to launch the CWI much more clearly, with public material appealing to the advanced workers.

But in the early 1990s we decided that we would open a dialogue with other international organisations. The collapse of Stalinism forced us to review our work and approach. Other organisations would be forced to change, we thought, and some of them did, but not always in a positive direction. Some of them moved in a rightward direction, while others, like the SWP in Britain, who we did approach for discussions, merely asserted that they had been right 'all along'. They were more successful, it seemed then, than the Socialist Party and the CWI in Britain. Militant had suffered a split. Inevitably, the fallout of that pushed us back. On the other hand, the SWP, with their theory of the '1930s in slow motion', were super-activists on the public arena with posters and a lot of noise.

They seemed to be everywhere but the SWP became synonymous with 'students with placards'. It was a kind of voluntarism, of trying to speak louder than your voice, attempting to appear more important than what you actually counted for within the working class. The SWP was largely a petty-bourgeois organisation, but with a certain layer of impatient workers as well, who thought all that was required was to proclaim the revolution. To some extent, they are still doing it on demonstrations with their slogan of "one solution, revolution". But when we opened up a discussion, we clashed with them and still do on a number of issues. We offered collaboration. Unfortunately, that broke down in the Socialist Alliance, where they wanted to impose their programme and their forms of organisation on what should have been a loose form of organisation.

We went to see the USFI and we opened up a dialogue and discussion with them. Bob Labi, Tony Saunois, Lynn Walsh and I all visited the USFI. I met Livio Maitan for the first time in many years. But it became clear to us that they were on a more opportunist trajectory, towards liquidation of the ideas of Trotskyism. We sent comrades to see the LIT. I have been to see the LIT in Brazil. Tony Saunois spoke at LIT conferences and so on. Our comrades in Brazil were at one stage part of their organisation with faction rights. So we went on a 'voyage of discovery' to see whether the political landscape had changed. Unfortunately, we found that, as far as other international organisations were concerned, it had not changed all that much.

Therefore, while we still keep our lines of communication open and we are still prepared to discuss and debate with these organisations, we have concentrated our efforts in the past period in building up the CWI and our membership, developing the ideas of the CWI. We now have organisations or individuals linked to the CWI in 34 countries. Some of them are substantial organisations with an implantation in the working-class movement and are factors in the life of the workers' movement, or in a particular section of the working class. In Britain, after quite a difficult period of the 1990s, we are building.

We have declined from the 8,000 members we had in the 1980s in the whole of Britain but we are still a formidable party with roots in the labour movement and approximately 2,000 members. But that is quite a commendable achievement on the basis of all the difficult objective factors that I mentioned before. We have maintained a very good older cadre who act as a lever for the next generation to develop. We have also recruited a substantial layer of new young comrades who are participating in the struggle. But we are also putting a certain amount of attention and time into developing them politically and theoretically. We have at the present time, in England and Wales, over 30 full-timers, most of them at our national centre, but with regional full-timers in Wales, in the Southwest of England, in Manchester, in the Northeast, in the West and East Midlands, and Yorkshire. At its height, Militant had 320 full-time workers for the party – some of them voluntary. Not all of them were paid a wage. Some of them were unemployed and were paid supplements. But that was an indication of the position that we had.

In Ireland, we have an important organisation with councillors and an MP. Our section in Germany has just come through the experience of the WASG with our comrade, Lucy Redler, standing as number one in the list of the Berlin WASG, getting 50,000 votes in Berlin. In Sri Lanka, our comrade Siri stood in the presidential elections last year for the USP and came third. This has given our party an important platform to intervene in the present situation.

In terms of membership, the CWI is one of the most important, if not the most important, of the Trotskyist internationals. We are still small in comparison with the international tasks that are posed by the period. We certainly have now more of an international basis. We are present on all continents and nearly all of the countries of Europe, although we only have a toehold in some. Southern Europe is unfortunately one of the weaknesses of the CWI, apart from Greece and now Cyprus, which we hope to overcome in the next period.

Relations within the CWI

Do the national sections have autonomy to decide their own policies? Is there continuous discussion with the International Secretariat (IS) of the International? What is the relationship of the politics and organisation of the sections?

We still accept that democratic centralism is vital for a revolutionary party. Even in a trade union or the workers' movement, forms of centralism exist. In the 1990s, because the term 'democratic centralism' was linked to Stalinism, we temporarily changed the terminology to 'democratic unity'. But we found this was inadequate. We defend the idea of democratic centralism but oppose bureaucratic centralism. Some other Trotskyist organisations have given a bad name to Leninism, Trotskyism and to democratic centralism. They pursue a form of bureaucratic centralism.

We have, in national sections and at international level a transparent democracy: the election of all officials and the right of recall. I am an elected official and other comrades in the leadership are elected officials of the International. There is the right of recall. If one quarter of the branches demands a special national conference, it has to be called. If one third of a Central Committee demand a special CC it has to be called. If a certain number of the sections demand a special World Congress, resources allowing, it has to be called. The World Congress is the highest authority of the CWI. We lean more towards democracy, autonomy and the development of independent national leaderships in the sections, rather than an overemphasis on centralism. This is necessary because of the bad experiences of Stalinist and social-democratic forms of organisations. The baleful influence of Stalinism has even infected some Trotskyist organisations as well.

In general, it is entirely wrong to resort to expulsions as a first reaction on policy issues, which has happened in some organisations but not in the CWI. Differences need to be discussed. In Scotland, we had a political split with the leadership of our then section in 1998. But we wanted them to stay in the International to argue their point of view even though they had broken a number of the political and organisational norms of our party. But they decided they could not stay.

Bob Labi: "In the discussions in 1998, we disagreed with what they were proposing – the political basis and how they were proposing, through the Scottish Socialist Party (SSP), effectively to liquidate the CWI section. We took no disciplinary action against them despite the fact we disagreed totally with what they did and how they have subsequently developed. In fact, they eventually left us, voluntarily, in 2001, precisely because we decided not to take disciplinary measures on this issue even though they had broken with our norms and traditions. Sometimes, when we have been unfortunately faced with corruption, for example, as within our group in Ukraine, we have taken disciplinary measures. We had no alternative.

"But in regard to Scotland (all the documents are published and in the public domain) we did not take any disciplinary measures because we were politically confident that, in time, we would be proved right, as has been revealed in the degeneration of the SSP since. But they left of their own volition, they were not forced out. I think this is linked to another point. Peter said in the 1990s we discussed with groups internationally and we did not reach agreement. In terms of how the CWI has developed in different countries, it has very often been through meeting and discussing with different groups or different parties, with which, over a period of time, we have found a common basis and they have joined us. It has been in a minority of cases where already existing members of the CWI have gone to different countries to set up CWI groups. Outside Europe, in Sri Lanka and in Nigeria, today's CWI sections come from the members of existing groups or parties, joining the CWI maybe 30 or 40 years ago.

"Presently, we are discussing with the Socialist Party of Malaysia which has its own history. It developed independently but we are discussing with it and the same is true for other countries. So the fact that we are not discussing with other international groupings at this present time does not mean that at a national level we are not discussing with different groupings. We have to see on what basis we can agree and what basis we disagree, and how relationships can develop, which sometimes can be over a long period of time before the issues become clear. It is not just discussion itself; it is experience, events, the development of the objective situation and our own activities".

Do you think of yourselves as an 'International' and, arising from this, do you think that the future leadership of an international revolution will emerge from an enlargement of the CWI?

We are an international organisation and, as I have previously explained, always took an internationalist approach, even when we had few forces outside of Britain. But, given the historical experience and the disappointments which have arisen from the failure of quite small organisations who proclaim themselves as 'the' International, we were against this when we established the CWI in 1974. We can point to the analysis that we have made historically and, particularly since 1991-92, as a correct description of the general political situation facing the working class and the conclusions which flowed from this.

That does not mean to say that we have been correct in every detail, that there have not been mistakes, for instance, on the likely tempo of events. The great socialist leaders like Marx himself, while correct in their general analysis, made many mistakes on timing. History has a way of confirming a perspective only after a delay and sometimes after considerable time. Because the political arena internationally is littered with self-proclaimed 'Internationals', we called ourselves the 'Committee *for* a Workers' International'. This implies that we need a new International which could begin to establish mass roots and the CWI will take the necessary steps, with others, to realise this.

Would this mass International be merely an 'enlargement of the CWI'? We are a small organisation that has sought to maintain the thread of genuine Trotskyist and Marxist ideas in one of the most difficult objective circumstances for maybe 100 years. There are some comparisons to be made with the position facing Marxists and Trotskyists since 1989 to that which confronted the Bolsheviks and Trotsky following the defeat of the 1905-07 revolution. In Russia, a period of reaction set in, accompanied by splits both to the right and the left, reflected within the Bolsheviks.

Of course, the Russian Marxists confronted much more brutal repression – executions, exile and persecution – than Marxists in general, certainly in advanced industrial countries, faced in the 1990s. But, even in the period of reaction of 1905 to 1911/12, the Russian workers' movement could still look towards the international horizon and see the rise of strong workers' parties and other organisations of the working class – in France, Germany, Italy, even in the US, where Eugene Debs got almost one million votes for a socialist programme in the US presidential elections in 1912. This was a source of encouragement and strength to them.

The present period has been of a more generalised worldwide ideological reaction, which has affected the workers' movement, almost without exception, on every continent and in practically every country. The ideas of socialism and their proponents, never mind Marxism and Trotskyism, have had to struggle just to maintain their existence against the background of a pro-capitalist, pro-market ideological barrage. This has had the effect of creating ideological confusion which has left its mark on even those who still claim to be Marxists and Trotskyists. Some have even abandoned their previous ideological standpoints, formal adherence to Trotskyist ideas, and have openly embraced a reformist perspective. In fact, the overwhelming majority of even radical intellectuals today subscribe to these ideas in one form or another.

Organisations and parties, formerly standing on the ultra-left (the IST/SWP in Britain and internationally, and fragments of the LIT) while maintaining certain sectarian practices – an intolerance towards other ideas, an unwillingness to debate discuss and open up dialogue – have shifted towards the right. Others have retreated into a sectarian *cul-de-sac*.

A major factor in this ideological confusion arises from the fact that in the recent period the proletariat in Europe, Japan and the US has not yet moved decisively onto the political arena. When they do, this will exercise a profound effect, not least on the confused ideological melange which constitutes the intellectual milieu of even those who consider themselves 'radicals' at the present time. So our answer is that a new mass International would not be just an 'enlargement' of the CWI, nor would it necessarily come from those proclaiming themselves to be Marxists and Trotskyists today. New formations of the working class and young people, splits of a sizeable character from reformist and centrist organisations, could develop and look towards a new mass International. These new fresh forces of the working class will constitute the overwhelming majority of a new mass International. We believe, however, that the CWI, as long as it maintains its clarity politically and dynamism organisationally, will be an important part of this process. In general, a mass

International will be built not in a linear fashion, of gradual accretions in support for the CWI or any other organisation, but by a combination of fusions between genuine Marxist forces and even of splits towards the left of sizeable workers' organisations and parties which will move towards a Marxist position."

There were many experiences from previous Internationals, which differed substantially from one another. The Fourth International, even when Trotsky was alive, was quite ineffective (apart from Vietnam and maybe the SWP in the US). Also there were many splits in many groups in what appeared to be an 'eternal war' with each other. The most serious attempt to build a mass revolutionary International was the 'Third'. The approach of Lenin was not sectarian. In Moscow, in the first congresses of the International, there was the participation of the centrist USPD, led by Kautsky, and the anarchist CNT trade union from Spain, as well as opportunist elements from the French Socialist Party such as Cachin, of anarcho-syndicalists like Rosmer and Serge, and also the International Workers of the World of 'Big Bill' Haywood. Do you think the future of a mass International needs to be a pure 'Trotskyist' International?

I answered part of your question above. I would not agree that the Fourth International launched by Trotsky was 'ineffective'. It did not manage to establish a mass base, largely because of the difficult objective factors which existed in the 1930s, during the Second World War and the situation I described earlier in the post-1945 period. The mistakes of those who were in the leadership after the murder of Trotsky played their part also. Nevertheless, the analysis by Trotsky of Stalinism and a whole number of other questions are indispensable political weapons for the new generations of workers to intervene in the struggles which are opening up. Without Trotsky's monumental contribution on the analysis of the Stalinist regimes, the generation of Marxists who followed him would have been at an enormous disadvantage. No doubt they would have found a way to a correct analysis and method but with many difficulties, false starts, barren detours and so on. The greatest contribution of Trotsky, as he himself conceded, was not the leading role he undoubtedly played in the Russian Revolution, but in his work of a theoretical character, which he undertook in the 1930s.

The idea of the Third International was first launched by Lenin against the background of the debacle of the First World War and the capitulation of the reformist and centrist leaders to social chauvinism. However, it only became realisable on the basis of the greatest event in human history, the Russian Revolution. This naturally attracted the support of the world working class and compelled all political formations within its ranks to adopt a position for or against the revolution.

Reformist and centrist leaders were compelled to display a certain sympathy because of the mood of the workers within their ranks. This meant that opportunists, disguised reformists and centrists, as well as genuine revolutionary fighters, some of whom came from anarcho-syndicalist backgrounds, such as Rosmer and Serge and the IWW, found a place in the ranks of the Third International.

Lenin, while he welcomed genuine class fighters, even if they did not agree necessarily with the Bolsheviks' rounded-out Marxist programme and approach, nevertheless adopted a different attitude towards opportunist leaders. These, he recognised, represented a potential danger, a corrosive reformist influence within the ranks of a revolutionary International. He was therefore compelled to expand the original requirements for member organisations to 21 until most of the reformist, opportunist leaders could find no place within the ranks of the Third International. Therefore, while Lenin welcomed all genuine mass and potential mass forces irrespective of their initial political positions, he, along with Trotsky, was nevertheless insistent on the Marxist, revolutionary character of the Third International.

Would a future mass International need to be a pure, 'Trotskyist' International? Whether it would be known by that name or not is not important. It is the political content, the programme and methods by which a new International is formed that is crucial. The terms 'Marxist', 'Leninist' or 'Trotskyist' denote for us the ideas of scientific socialism applied to the modern era. No matter how old an idea or body of ideas, if they are the best in explaining the character of the modern era and the tasks of the workers' movement, then they are the most 'topical' and current. At the same time, it cannot be ruled out that there would be certain transitional forms of international organisations before arriving at the idea of a mass Marxist International. We seek to collaborate with others in order to take the workers' movement in general forward, as well as discussing with and joining together with the genuine forces of Trotskyism where there is general political agreement.

In your brief history of the CWI you said that there are conscious, good revolutionary comrades internationally, workers and youth, who are presently outside the CWI. What do you consider are the conditions for the fusion or unification with other groups or parties?

There are many good revolutionary forces worldwide who are not CWI members or sympathisers or, in some cases, do not even know about the CWI. We would collaborate with all of these forces on concrete issues and seek to open up a discussion, debate and dialogue, which is absolutely essential in this period for clarifying the tasks of the workers' movement internationally. It is not possible to lay down in advance and in every circumstance the conditions for fusion or unification with other groups or parties. Where we can arrive at ideological agreement on the main issues, then the CWI would be open and welcoming to all those who wish to join our ranks. However, given the background I have mentioned earlier of political and ideological confusion, it would be wrong to rush into this without the ground being properly prepared. This means, in general, discussion, an attempt to work together in practice, and common campaigns on crucial issues, both within countries and internationally. We have joined together with groups who were initially not Trotskyist. I give examples of this in the history of the CWI. At present, we are discussing with important organisations such as the Socialist Party of Malaysia. We do not have agreement with them on a number of issues but we have friendly collaborative relations, with invitations to speak at each other's meetings in the hope of clarification and possible agreement politically, which hopefully would have organisational conclusions. However, even if a fusion or unification is not possible with some groups, there is no reason why collaboration would not be possible.

In recent years, in a lot of the material of the CWI, you have spoken of the 'long night' of the 1990s but that socialism is now coming back onto the agenda. The world is in turmoil but you hear from many people that 'socialism is a good idea but, unfortunately, it is utopian'. Others say that 'socialism does not work because human nature is too egoistic'. Do you think, after the tragic experience of Stalinism, that socialism in the real sense of the term could work and solve many of the problems of humanity? Can socialism as a system work?

We have answered these questions many times in our publications and in books such as Hannah Sell's *Socialism in the 21st Century*, in *Socialism Today* in a series of articles, and in the publications of the sections of the CWI. I will give a brief summary here. The ideological reaction of which I have spoken dominated the 1990s, although the working class did attempt to struggle in big movements. Now, because of the experience of 20 years of neo-liberalism and its clear failure, especially in the neo-colonial world, a shift has taken place, which has put socialism back on the agenda. Even the fact that Chávez in Venezuela moved from a position of 'humanitarian capitalism' to proclaiming the need for 'socialism' is an indication of what is taking place. In Europe as well, there is a layer of young people – not a substantial force at this stage, but important – which is searching for socialist ideas. Many of them have become Marxists through observing the situation, reading and looking at events internationally.

Nevertheless, there is still in this situation an element of the 1990s in the scepticism displayed towards socialist ideas. The memory of Stalinism is still there as a certain barrier to the genuine ideas and forces of Marxism. Some, even good young people, say initially that 'socialism is utopian', that it does not work, as the experiences of Russia and Eastern Europe indicate. In this sense, we have a more difficult job than even the generation of socialists and revolutionaries before the First World War. Socialism was then a grandiose idea to be put into practice in the future. The Russian Revolution realised this dream and reverberated around the planet, in the 'ten days that shook the world'. But then we had Stalinism.

Reinforced by hostile capitalist propaganda, the impression has been given that 'socialism has had its day', and it is necessary to try more 'radical' ideas. This is accompanied by the age-old argument against socialism that human beings are too 'egoistic' or 'individualistic' to act in common, in a collective or altruistic fashion, to change society. History has shown that this is wrong, as evidenced by not just the Russian Revolution but the numerous attempts at revolution made by the working class and the poor in the 20th century which failed due to faulty leadership. The mass of the population will not look for an alternative until the present system is evidentially and clearly breaking down. This is not true of the combative, courageous minority who are looking for explanations and can find a way to socialism and Marxism now. As we explained above, the boom of the 1990s and the earlier part of this decade has not yet exhausted itself. It will take great events – and they are coming, not least through the economic difficulties of capitalism – to shake off the lingering illusions that this system can be 'reformed' and rendered more 'humane'.

Even when there is a rupture, the masses will not necessarily always turn to 'socialism' first because of the experiences of the past. They will ransack the 'storerooms of history', embrace 'easier' attempts from the past as examples for change. In these conditions, reformist ideas and parties built on them can grow. Centrist formations could also develop, especially in the neo-colonial world, with the objective conditions facing the masses worsening and becoming unbearable. Experience is the greatest teacher of humankind. Having exhausted these false paths, not at once and not all together, the masses will look for a socialist alternative. However, this movement will not be a simple repetition of the past nor will the parties that fight for socialism merely be a replication of what has gone before. New fresh layers moving into action will throw up all kinds of innovative, imaginative ideas but socialism as a broad concept will become a mass force. Karl Marx once said that when an idea grips the minds of the masses it becomes a material force. This we saw in the Russian Revolution and also will be witnessed again in the colossal events which impend in Britain, Italy and worldwide.

socialist books

All of the books listed below are available from Socialist Books. To order further copies of this publication or any from either the list or the many other publications published by Socialist Books contact us at:

Socialist Books, PO Box 24697, London E11 1YD
telephone: 020 8988 8789 or email: socialistbooks@socialistparty.org.uk
or online at the socialist books **website: www.socialistbooks.co.uk**

recent titles available from socialist books

- **A Socialist World is Possible:**
  The History of the CWI
  by Peter Taaffe
  Published August 2004. 96 pages paperback
  An account and celebration of the activity and contribution of the Committee for a Workers International (CWI) on the 30 Anniversary of its founding, showing how the role and influence of the organisation has developed and change -, in some regions of the world quite dramatically - from its humble origins.
  Price £5.00

- **1926 General Strike**
  Workers Taste Power
  by Peter Taaffe
  Published May 2006. 192 pages paperback
  Written to commemorate the eightieth anniversary of the 1926 General Strike in Britain and, more importantly, to draw the lessons from this movement.
  Price £7.50

- **Empire Defeated - Vietnam War:**
  The lessons for today
  by Peter Taaffe
  Published February 2004. 128 pages paperback
  A history of the Vietnam War drawing out the lessons to be learnt from this conflict, especially in the aftermath of the Iraq war.
  Price £6.00

other titles available
from socialist books

- **Pamphlet: Join the Campaign for a New Workers' Party** by The Socialist Party
  Published February 2006. 36 pages paperback
  A brief explanation of why the Socialist Party has initiated the Campaign for a New Workers' Party.
  Price £1.00

- **A Civil War without Guns:**
  20 Years On: the lessons of the 1984-85 Miners' Strike by Ken Smith
  Published May 2004. 128 pages paperback
  A balance sheet of this important struggle. Price £5.00

- **Socialism in the 21st Century:**
  The Way Forward for Anti-Capitalism
  by Hannah Sell.
  Published August 2002. New Updated Edition February 2006. 96 pages paperback
  An essential read for all anti-capitalists, trade union activists and socialists.
  Price £5.00

- **Che Guevara: Symbol of Struggle** by Tony Saunois.
  Published September 2005. 96 pages paperback
  An appraisal of the life and role of Che Guevara as a revolutionary.
  Price £5.00

- **Cuba: Socialism and Democracy:**
  Debates on the Revolution and Cuba Today by Peter Taaffe.
  Published 2000. 128 pages paperback
  Defence of the Socialist Party's analysis of the Cuban revolution.
  Price £5.00

- **The Rise of Militant: Militant's 30 years** by Peter Taaffe.
  Published 1995. 570 pages paperback
  Story of Militant, forerunner of the Socialist Party (English and Welsh section of the CWI), from its birth.
  Price £10.99

- **Liverpool - A City that Dared to Fight** by Tony Mulhearn and Peter Taaffe.
  Published 1988, 500 pages paperback
  Militant led Liverpool city council's battle against the Thatcher government 1983-1997.
  Price £7.95

the socialist party

join us

I would like to find out more about / join the Socialist Party ❑

Name

Address

Postcode

Tel No   Email

Trade Union (if applicable)

If you are interested in finding out more about the Socialist Party
or our publications simply fill in this form and return to:
Socialist Party, PO Box 24697, London E11 1YD
email: join@socialistparty.org.uk tel: 020 8988 8767
website: **www.socialistparty.org.uk**

the socialist

weekly paper of the Socialist Party

Get your copy of **the socialist** delivered regularly by
subscribing. There is a special introductory offer of 10
issues for only £6.00.

subscription rates:
- 12 issues: £9.00
- 6 months: £18.00
- 1 year: £36.00

You can telephone for either a direct debit form or pay by
credit card on: **020 8988 8796**
the address to contact about subscriptions and international rates is: **Socialist Party - Subscriptions,
PO Box 24697, London E11 1YD**

Contacting the Committee for a Workers' International

The Committee for a Workers' international has affiliated parties and organisations in more than 35 countries, on all continents. The way to contact our comrades differs from country to country. Some you can contact directly. For others, it is easier to do it via the CWI office in London, just e-mail to the International Office of the CWI: cwi@worldsoc.co.uk or contact us at PO Box 3688, London, Ell 1YE, Britain. Telephone: + 44 (0)20 8988 8760. Fax: + 44 (0)20 8988 8793. Visit our website at: http://www.socialistworld.net

If you want to know more about us in Denmark, Finland, Kashmir, Luxembourg, Spain or anywhere else ... then contact the CWI international office above.

Australia: Socialist Party.
PO Box 1015, Collingwood, Victoria 3066.
phone: + 61 3 9650 0160;
e-mail: info@socialistpartyaustralia.org

Austria: Sozialistische Linkspartie.
Kaiserstrasse 14/11, 1070 Wien.
phone: + 43 1 524 6310;
fax: + 43 1 817 495 514 64;
e-mail: slp@slp.at

Belgium: LSP/MAS. PO Box10011,
1190 Vorst 3;
phone: + 322 3456181;
e-mail: lspmas@skynet.be

Brazil: Socialismo Revolucionario. Caixa
Postal 02009, CEP 01060-970, Sao Paulo
S.P. phone: + 55 11 3101 5646
e-mail: sr-cio@uol.com.br

Canada: Socialist Alternative. 903-633
Bay Street, Toronto, Ontario, MSG 2G4
e-mail: cwicanada@gmail.com

Chile: Socialismo Revolucionario,
Celso C Campos, Casilla 50310,
Correo Central, Santiago.
phone: + 56 2 622 9004;
e-mail: jandresverra@hotmail.com

CIS: 125167 Moscow a\Ya 37, Moscow.
e-mail: pabgem@online.ru

Cyprus:
Agias elenis 36, Galaxias center, ap.407
PO Box 1061, Nicosia.
e-mail:
youthagainstnationalism@gmail.com

Czech Republic: Socialistická
Alternativa - Budoucnost.
ul. V háji 4, 170 00 Praha 7 - Hole_ovice,
e-mail: budoucnost@email.cz

England & Wales: Socialist Party,
PO Box 24697, London E11 1YD
phone: + 44 20 8988 8777.
fax: + 44 20 8988 8787:
e-mail: campaigns@socialistparty.org.uk

France: Gauche révolutionnaire
Les amis de L'Egalite. Centre 166, 82 rue
Jeanne d'Arc, 76000 Rouen.
e-mail: grcontact@hotmail.org

Germany: Sozialistische Alternative.
Littenstraße 106/107, 10179 Berlin.
phone: + 49 30 2472 3802;
e-mail: info@sav-online.de

Greece: Xekinima.
8 Gortynos Street, PO Box 11254 Athens.
phone/fax: + 30 210 228 3018;
e-mail: xekinima@hotmail.com

India: Dudiyora Horaata.
PO Box 1828, Bangalore 560018.
e-mail: dudiyorahoraata@usnl.net

Ireland North: Socialist Party.
15 Lombard Street, Belfast BT1 1RB
phone: + 44 (0)2890 232962;
fax: + 44 (0)2890 311778;
e-mail: socialist@belfastsp.freeserve.co.uk

Ireland South: Socialist Party.
PO Box 3434, Dublin 8.
phone/fax: + 353 1 677 25 92;
e-mail: info@socialistparty.net

Israel/Palestine: Maavak Sozialisti
P.O. Box 5342, Tel Aviv 61053.
e-mail: info@maavak.org.il

Italy: Lotta per il Socialismo
e-mail: lottaperilsoc@hotmail.com

Japan: Kokusai Rentai
Kanayamachi Biru 3F, Kita-ku,
Temma 2-1-17 Osaka-shi 530-0043
e-mail: kokusairentai@hotmail.com

Netherlands: Offensief.
PO Box 11561, 1001 GN Amsterdam.
e-mail: info@offensief.nl

New Zealand:
e-mail: socialist_alternative@hotmail.com

Nigeria: Democratic Socialist Movement.
PO Box 2225, Agege, Lagos.
tel: +234 1 804 6603 or
+ 234 803 712 7929
e-mail: dsmcentre@hotmail.com

Pakistan: Socialist Movement Pakistan
tel: +92 333 433 1755
e-mail: revolutionary1917@yahoo.com

Poland: Grupa na Rzecz Partii
Robotniczej
e-mail: ebsgpr@wp.pl

Portugal: Alternativa Socialista.
Apartado 27018, 1201-950, Lisboa
e-mail: alternativasocialista@gmail.com

Scotland: CWI. PO Box 6773, Dundee,
DD1 1YL. phone: + 44 1382 833 759;

South Africa: Democratic Socialist
Movement. PO Box 596, Newton, 2113,
Johannesburg. phone: + 27 11 342 2220;
e-mail: democraticsocialist@mweb.co.za

Sri Lanka: United Socialist Party.
44/10 Pichchamalwatta, Nawala Road
Narahenpita, Colombo 5
phone: + 94 1 1451 0289
e-mail: usp@sltnet.lk

Sweden: Rattvisepartiet Socialisterna.
PO Box 73; 123 03 Farsta. phone: + 46 8
605 9400. fax: + 46 8 556 252 52;
e-mail: rs@socialisterna.org

USA: Socialist Alternative.
PO Box 45343, Seatlle, W4, 98145.
e-mail: info@socialistalternative.org

Index